CORNWALL

Edited by Dave Thomas

First published in Great Britain in 1999 by
POETRY NOW YOUNG WRITERS
Remus House, Coltsfoot Drive,
Woodston,
Peterborough, PE2 9JX
Telephone (01733) 890066

HB ISBN 0 75430 401 9
SB ISBN 0 75430 402 7

FOREWORD

This year, the Poetry Now Young Writers' Kaleidoscope competition proudly presents the best poetic contributions from over 32,000 up-and-coming writers nationwide.

Successful in continuing our aim of promoting writing and creativity in children, each regional anthology displays the inventive and original writing talents of 11-18 year old poets. Imaginative, thoughtful, often humorous, *Kaleidoscope Cornwall* provides a captivating insight into the issues and opinions important to today's young generation.

The task of editing inevitably proved challenging, but was nevertheless enjoyable thanks to the quality of entries received. The thought, effort and hard work put into each poem impressed and inspired us all. We hope you are as pleased as we are with the final result and that you continue to enjoy *Kaleidoscope Cornwall* for years to come.

CONTENTS

Nathan John Oliver	86
Mark Hosking	86
Luke Howes	87
Ashley Jephson	87
Lauren Henderson	88
Mark Clay	88
Fenny Potts	89
Sara Graham	90
Natasha Kearey	90
Mahala Martin	91
Sarah-Jane Kewn	91
Bryony Davidson	92
Casvelyn James	93
Clare Laity	94
Lucy Stubbings	94
Charlotte Louise Lodey	95
Natalie Boyns	96
Alison Pring	96
Toni Spurrier	97
Samantha Lowes	97
Tracy Attridge	98
Neil Mainwaring	98
Laura Jackson	99
Lewis Barr	100
Sally Georgina Titus	100
Jade Jenkins	101
Sophie Richards	102
Kane Whitley	102
Josh Harris	103
Lasalle Simon	103
Daniel Williams	104
Claire Graham	104
Morwenna Matthews	105
Patricia Gee	105
Lucy Burgan	106
Jess Croucher	106
Laurens Everitt	107
Zach James Wooley	107

The Poems

I HATE BOYS

I hate boys they are
so bad,
I hate boys they are
so sad.
I hate boys they are
such drags,
But sometimes they
are so nice,
They love themselves,
They are such brags.

Abi Humphries (11)

OCEAN

The ocean is big,
The ocean is green,
The ocean is kind,
The ocean is mean.
Many miles across,
Many miles below,
Sometimes my friend,
Sometimes my foe.
With waves enormous
All frothy and curled,
The Atlantic, the Pacific -
The lions' share of the world.

Laura Miller (12)

THE UNSINKABLE QUEEN OF THE SEA

On April tenth 1912 she glided out of port
With great excitement on the quay
Titanic was bound for New York
The unsinkable Queen of the Sea.

With two thousand plus passengers on board
Villains and rogues in the lower decks
The upper class drinking their tea
The unsinkable Queen of the Sea.

Five days out in the darkening gloom
Struck an iceberg that shouldn't be there
The maiden met her doom
The unsinkable Queen of the Sea.

With not enough lifeboats to save them all
One thousand five hundred souls died
The rich and the famous
But mainly the poor
The unsinkable Queen of the Sea.

Jael Valerio (12)

LIKE DIAMONDS

An empty house on an isolated island,
Overlooking the ocean,
glistening and sparkling like sailing diamonds
Gliding and colliding with the furious wind,
humpback whales sing their morning song
as it wakes up the sleepy sea bed,
seaweed waves like sleek and silent sea serpents,
forced to dance and sway with the current,
soon another busy day will begin in the marine world.

Roxanne Reeves (13)

RAINBOW

Red is the sign that draws my attention,
Red is the book that I care to mention.
Orange is the sun, so fiery and hot,
Orange is the pencil with which I draw a dot.
Yellow is the pansy a sweet-smelling flower;
Yellow is the colour of wealth and of power.
Green is the field that holds many sheep,
Green is the ditch that is so, so deep.
Blue is the sky drifting in the breeze,
Blue is the ocean settling at ease.
Indigo is the dark mysterious night,
Indigo is the colour more interesting than white.
Violet is the gown of a rich lady,
Violet is the bed sheet for a small baby.

Rainbows are colourful and cannot be sold,
And at the end of one you might just find *gold!*

Stephanie Todd (12)

EERILY

Eerily a wolf cries in the night
Eerily a lamp shines its dim light
Eerily a fox hunts in the town
Eerily a snowflake falls to the ground.

Eerily a footstep is heard on the stair
Eerily an old woman rocks in her chair
Eerie is a witch
But eeriest of all,
Is an old ghost standing in your hall.

Sam Moody (12)

FISHY FRIENDS

A fish, whose name was Fred
Was always in his sea bed
He was always asleep
And he lived in the deep
And his nose was very bright red.

Fred's friend, who was a cow
Could never understand how
Whilst stood still all day
He would hear people say
'Hey there, how, now, brown cow!'

Fred's uncle, a shark, with no fear
Said 'Oh dear, isn't it queer?
I was basking one day
In the middle of May
And my head banged on the banjo pier!'

Fred hated a seagull called Lee
He said 'He's always smiling at me
The sight of his beak
Makes me feel weak
'Cos I know he wants me for tea!'

A jellyfish said 'Here's a thing
I feel like I'm going to sing.
If you ask me to stop
I'll get in a strop
And show you the strength of my sting!'

A fisherman's name, it was John
Said 'I'm going to tempt Fred with a scone
I'll attach it right here
And drop it quite near
But it was too late Fred had gone!'

Sam Lee (12)

FAR AWAY THOUGHTS

Over the hills in a far away land,
where the sun doesn't reach and tall trees stand.
Birds fly high in the mist broken sky.
A child sleeps, a child lies.

Down by the stream in a far away land,
where the grasses are tall and the cornflowers stand.
Field mice scatter, in the gloom of the night.
A lady and baby lie in moonlight.

Deep in the forest in a far away land,
where the old oak rustles and people are banned.
Wolves prowl about in the cold morning air.
A man lies dying without a care.

Alexandra Farah (12)

PEACEFULLY

Peacefully the pianist plays,
Peacefully the daffodil sways,
Peacefully the kite glides in the sky,
Peacefully the violet hides, shy.

Peacefully the gulls soar across the bay,
Peacefully the calf lies in the hay,
Peace is the moment when baby lays down her head -
But the most peaceful thing of all is lying in bed!

Sarah Goldsworthy (12)

GIRLS V BOYS

Girls go nitter natter
Boys go chitter chatter

Girls like to make themselves pretty
Boys think they're very witty

Girls try and look like a flower
Boys are waiting for the shower

Girls think they're very bright
Boys gang up and fight

Girls sing and dance to songs
Boys all think they are very strong

Girls are very neat
Boys - all they do is eat

Girls dress like a fairy
Boys' heads are light and airy

Girls wear a short skirt
Boys hang around and flirt

Girls sometimes are silly
Boys can be a bully

Girls like eating sweets
Boys can be very sweet.

Emma Cudlipp (12)

UNTITLED

Standing on the blocks,
Butterflies in my stomach,
Dolphin kicks with splashing feet
Is what I aim for in today's swim meet.

Bang! Goes the gun,
Away we all go,
Plunging into the water,
On a very long journey.

Powering arms for every stroke
Gasping for air on each breath
Feeling as slow as a sloth
When will this end? Tell me the truth.

The final length,
Going all out
Each stroke gets more painful
And at last, out of breath
I stretch my last stroke.

The other competitors
Struggle to the end,
What a glorious feeling
To finish before them.

Standing on the podium
Gold medal over my head
My efforts rewarded
All worthwhile in the end.

Lynda Flanaghan (13)

WHO AM I?

Who am I?
Where did I come from?
How did I get here?
And where am I?

Those were the questions floating around my dark empty head,

Did I hurt someone?
Did someone hurt me?
Why do I feel like someone is after me?

Suddenly I had an urge to walk south.

Why south?
Am I running from someone?
Or to someone?
Or maybe both?

Mandy Pendray (12)

LOVE

My love for Beth is so strong I can taste it,
I'd give her my heart and make them take it out so I could feel it,
I know her smell like I know my age,
I love her warm and gentle touch,
I know when I see her the grin on her face, cheeky and cheerful,
not a scrap of disgrace,
I could not live without her,
I love her so dear,
She's my little sister and she's why I'm here.

Sarah Bird (12)

SPACEMAN!

At half past ten,
Late last night,
I thought I'd get up,
For a quick bite,
I turned on the light,
And to my surprise,
I saw some bright green,
Glowing eyes,
I screamed for my mum,
She came running quick,
I said spaceman,
Look there quick quick,
She said,
Now turn out the light,
And don't get a fright,
If they come and see you again,
Just scream for me,
And I'll come and see,
And tell you to get to bed
Again!

Emma Taylor (12)

THE MOON

He's there, when you want him.
He's there, when you don't.
He hides in the clouds when they are afloat.
He's there, in the morning when the sun is out.
He's there, in the evening when the stars are about.
He's there, at night-time shining on the town.
He's there, in the sky with his passionate frown.

Melissa Mardle (12)

MY CAT

We have a cat called Thomas,
Who is truly loved by all of us.

By the time you count to three,
He can be up a tree.

Once he caught a little mouse,
And it was running round the house.

He gets wicked at night,
Which is quite a sight.

His tail he will chase,
At an incredible pace.

When he's calmed down,
He does not make a sound.

He sits in our garage all nice and cosy,
Looking out to see if he can spot Rosie.

And that's why we love our cat Thomas.

Lynessa Hancock (12)

FRIENDS

Friends are forever,
like the wind, rain and sea,
Friends are forever,
Together you and me.

Friends are forever,
like the trees, sand and sky,
Friends are forever,
Together till they die.

Laura Allsey (12)

FOOD

Food, from the great spices of the Earth that give a feeling of
luxury and make our mouths tingle,
To the sweet fruits of far, exotic lands where tanned peaches
ripen in the heat, and sway in the warm breeze.

Existing in so many forms, food the flesh of another creature,
To the great trees that bear brightly coloured fruit.

Some believe the most fragile things in life are greatly
moulded pottery, or glass sculptures.
But I believe that the most delicate things are the food chains in
the animal kingdom, consisting of up to a thousand forms of life,
And the extinction of one species means certain death for
all the species.

Food the life giver, food the world's greatest treasure.

Daniel Matthews (12)

UNDER THE SEA

Far down on the sea floor,
Old wrecks which divers explore,
Covered in barnacles and crustaceans
The salty sea water causing disintegration.

Mackerel, dogfish, plaice and dabs,
And many different types of crabs,
Explore the sea bed,
Of seaweed and shells and bits of old ships,
As heavy as lead.

Old rusty anchors, lengths of chain,
Treasure sought for but in vain,
Many have probed deep in the depths of the sea,
Yet still it remains a mystery.

Cherry Martin (12)

TEACHERS

Why are all teachers the same,
They always try to pass the blame,
They seem to always want to shout,
When you don't even know what it's about.

Sure we might want to learn,
But why is it never our turn?
They want to rant and rave,
And tell us to behave.

We just have to get on with our work,
There is never a quirk.
Sometimes they're a bit stressy,
And tell you off for being messy.

But after all they're not that bad,
They're just a bit sad.

Rebecca Eatough (12)

THE SEA

The sea can be wild,
The sea can be calm,
The sea is so beautiful,
And can do a lot of harm.

The sea is so lovely,
Glistening in the sun,
Being by the sea
Is a great place to have fun.

As the boats glide in the harbour,
For their night's rest,
The seagulls are crying loud,
As the harbour looks its best.

> The sun rises over the sea,
> As the waves pound upon the shore,
> The waves smash against the rocks,
> As the boats go out once more.

Katie Skinner (12)

SHADOW

I have a little friend,
Who follows me around,
He doesn't stand up,
He stays right on the ground,
He is a very quiet friend,
And never talks at all,
But in the dark and in the light,
He grows short and tall,
Right by my side,
Is where my friend does stay,
Always right next to me,
Every single day,
My little friend has a name,
I think you might like to know,
I call my little faithful friend,
My Shadow.

Nina Saada (12)

THE MYSTERIOUS MOON

The moon is a circle high up in the sky,
Some say it's cheese but I don't know why!
If you could taste it would it be like cheese pie?
    I don't think so.

The moon has a colour, the colour is white,
Some say that it's the master of the night.
    I don't think so.

Some say the cow jumped over the moon,
Some say the dish ran away with the spoon.
    I don't think so!

The moon spins round and around
Some say one day it will fall to the ground
    I don't think so!

The moon has lots of craters made by asteroids,
Some say when they hit it didn't make much noise.
    I don't think so.

Some people want to walk on the moon,
Some hope they can do this quite, quite soon.
    I don't think so.

Some say the moon is cold and mysterious,
Others say it is hot and glorious.
    I don't think so because I know . . .

The moon is just God's little bit of fun,
bouncing his silver ball reflecting off the sun.

Holly Spring (12)

NIGHT HORSE

Black as a crow
Dark as night
He gallops fast,
Faster than light.

His movements smooth
As he gallops on,
His tail silken soft
Shimmers like the sun.

His hooves strike the air
And never the ground,
As he gallops fast
Without a sound.

He lifts his head
Neighs loud and clear,
He is all courage,
With no fear.

With fiery eyes,
Kicks up his hooves
Melts into the shadows,
and the night horse is gone.

I stand at my window
And watch every night
To see the night horse,
Fast and in flight.

Eloise Higginson (12)

TREEN

In summertime
the sun shines down on Treen.
Tourists are here,
red like cooked lobsters.
The shop is open,
ice lollies go down well.
The campsite gets too full.
But as the holidays and tourists go,
the village is quiet.
Autumn falls and the mists come down,
the foghorn can once again be heard.
The camp shop closes,
the holiday houses stand empty
and look like they are sleeping.
Crops are no longer seen over the hedges,
grass is put into bales,
calves turned to cows ready for milking.
Harvest auction
and Hallowe'en parties,
children running around.
'Trick or treat,
5p or a sweet!'
Now the villagers' life begins.

Rachel Oldcorn (13)

MY DOG IS AN ALIEN

My dog is an alien, he made the bowl rise off
the floor.
My dog is an alien, he asked me for more.
My dog is an alien, he flew around the room,
My dog is an alien, he went *kaboom!*

Mark Hall (13)

NIGHTMARES

Nightmares are evil
Nightmares are bad
Some can be scary
Some can be sad.
You can be chased by a dog
Bitten by a snake.
When all of a sudden
It's over and you're awake.
You're scared to sleep
You want to dream
Your imagination runs riot.
It's all dark and so quiet
You break into a sweat
You just can't forget
The awful images
Which bring forward your fears
It's your . . .
                                    . . . *nightmare!*

Tamar Bates (13)

ALIEN

My mother's been acting all weird
She seems to be growing a beard
I've come to a conclusion
This is not an illusion
It's all become worse than I feared.

The strangest thing I've seen,
Is my mum has been turning green.
I noticed the odd shape of her head
One morning while lying in bed
I'm beginning to hope it's a dream.

Remy Dickson (12)

ALIEN

I was an alien.
I was such a girl,
Everybody laughed at me
Because I was ten feet tall.
My hair was green.
My feet were tiny.
I was scared,
Nobody would play with me.
I come from planet Mars,
Teachers were mad.
Dogs bit me all the time.
I had loads of friends before
I was an alien,
Now I have no friends at all.
My family were frightened of me,
I'm only a little girl,
I wish I was normal again,
Like everybody else.

Melissa Phillips (11)

BLACKBOARD HELL

Every day I come in my class
I see the blackboard with a border of brass,
It looks so boring,
Even when you're drawing.
So one night
I crept in with all my might!
And took the blackboard with lots of delight.

Kelly Smart (11)

ONE FINE DAY

One fine day
In the middle of the night.
Two dead men got up to fight
Two blind men
To see fair play.
Two dumb men
To shout hooray.

Back to back
They faced each other
Drew their swords
And shot each other.

A paralysed donkey was walking by
Kicked the blind man in the eye
Threw a stone brick wall in to a dry ditch
And drowned them all.

David Hall (11)

ALONE IN PENZANCE

I travelled on foot past school.
Memories being muttered to myself.
Giving thought to myself
Silence is not golden.
I wish someone would speak to me
Everything is free.
Don't care enough anymore
Tap tap tap having nothing but me
I'm scared
The world as we know it is ending.

Tom Maddern (13)

NOBODY'S THERE

I walk and walk from Heamoor to Penzance
It's so quiet
So many cars in weird places
All the shops are empty
The memories of Saturday
The people have gone

      Nobody's there

Crying babies
Annoyed parents
What's happened to them?

      Nobody's there

All by myself
The memories of friends
My family has gone

      They have all gone

Animals roam the streets
The owners have gone

      Nobody's there

I stroll into shops
There are no shop assistants
No one to help
All the things are there

      Nobody's there

I walk down Market Jew St
And down to the harbour
The boats are there
But like everywhere else

Nobody's there.

Claire Sharp (13)

IF I WERE THE HEAD TEACHER . . .

If I were the head teacher
I'd never tell you off
If you'd forgotten your homework -
I really would be soft.

I'd say 'I'll let you off this time,
But never do it again.'
If I caught them saying that their
Teacher really was insane.

I'd make sure they'd be good as gold,
And always had neat writing,
But the time when I'd get really annoyed
Is when they all start fighting!

Games would really be good fun,
And we would always run races,
In drama we would do great plays,
And in art, paper maché faces!

I think I'd be a great head teacher
But it would be quite odd,
Always having the same school dinners,
And deputising God!

Rebecca Gibson (11)

IF I WAS YOUR HEADMASTER

If I was your headmaster,
I would make your life a disaster,
Your day would start at seven,
Without a break till eleven.

If I was your headmaster,
I would make you work faster,
So that your workload is more,
You'll be dropping to the floor.

Break times will be few,
With barely time to use the loo,
Listen for the hometime bell,
Because that's the end of your daytime hell.

Run along home to Daddy and Mummy
Gobble up your tea that's really yummy
Sleep tight and dream all is well,
Remember what waits - your daytime hell.

Alisun Sisley (12)

IF I WAS NOT AN ALIEN!

If I was not an alien,
do you know what I'd be?
I would be an astronaut,
that is what I'd be,
and everyday people would say,
You've been to the moon,
you've been to Mars,
and you've seen a million stars.

Danielle Barr (12)

MY MUM AND DAD ARE ALIENS

My mum and dad are aliens,
I'm really really sure,
They're always acting weirdly,
And stamping on the floor.

They never go to sleep at night,
They run around the room,
And every time I say something,
They hit me with a spoon.

I said to them you're aliens,
You're ugly, green and old,
And then I saw some flashing lights
And everything went cold.

A big spaceship had landed.
My mum and dad were ready
To take off in a saucer
And go to Medileady.

Peter Penfold (12)

THE HEAD TEACHER WAS MEAN

The head teacher was always mean,
He made us run cross country,
He said we were lazy,
He made us do spelling tests,
And shouted because we got them all wrong.
One day when I'm a teacher,
Maybe I'll think the same,
Or maybe I'll be worse,
And even use the cane.

Rebecca Matthews (11)

LONELY

Walking down the street
With no one to meet
Lonely, lonely
Walking in a shop
There's no one there
No video cameras to stare
And I realise I'm on my own
Lonely, lonely

Going to school
Oh what a fool
I can't it's closed
Lonely, lonely
Getting very sad
And very mad
Just because there's no one there
Lonely, lonely.

Tom Curnow (13)

SNAILS

Why are snails so slow?
People may step on them you never know
On your flowers they always leave slime
With poems on snails it's hard to make them rhyme.

When I was little I collected about ten,
I stepped on them all but wouldn't do it again

Snails are sweet and also tiny
They are very delicate and also slimy,
I do like them very much
But they don't like it when they are touched.

Jenna Parsons (13)

SILENCE

No cars moving,
Everything still.
Hush around me - no thrill
Shops empty,
Pavements lifeless
Dogs, cats roaming at their will.

Silence everywhere -
World wiped out.
The only one with any clout.
Totally shocked
Astounded too
No point in trying to shout.

Just walking around
Feeling sad
Memories only keep out the bad.
What of the future?
Everything grim
Gone the good life I once had.

Toby Travers (13)

THE LION

Roar!
The lion walked slowly towards me.
His eyes met with mine.
Fear had struck.
His golden coloured mane, shook gently in the wind.
He yawned but it looked like he was saying
'Look at my big teeth.'
His padded feet seemed to thump as he walked
Up and down the wooden floor of his cage.

Rebecca Tracz (11)

MY MUM AND DAD ARE ALIENS

My mum and dad are aliens
I'm sure it's plain to see
Their habits are strange and unnatural
They're nothing at all like me!

My dad has got no hair on top
He says he's going bald
I'm sure he's picking up messages
From the planet he has called.

My mum has got strange powers
She's got eyes in the back of her head
She always seems to find out
What I've done and what I've said.

My mum and dad are aliens
They come from the planet Mars
Now I know my family tree
Grows beyond the stars.

Nicky Cox (14)

THE PLAGUE! THAT HIT PENZANCE

By myself in a forlorn world,
As I walk through the streets
Emptiness in my mind,
A single miaow from a cat,
Shop shut but still left open,
Cars parked,
Few animals dead,
Loneliness.

Emma Bryant (13)

SILENCE

Silence
No noise far or near,
Can't see anyone anywhere,
Except in my head,
My memories appear,
Stillness as I walk around,
Don't know whether to laugh or frown,
I heard a bird and looked up
Into the sky that was blue,
I thought your family and friends
Are looking at you,
Loneliness
I hope I get out of this place,
I'll promise that I'll always
Say grace,
Nobody here,
      Not a trace.

Anneka Ladner (13)

SILENCE

I stroll down the street of emptiness, no sound around.
Lonely, sad, deserted by my friends.
My heart is still filled with sensational daydreaming thoughts.
Dogs, cats all around just the sound of
my feet tapping the ground.

The moon, stars above my head are close to me,
Like some unwanted devil.
The wind whistling in my ear, just the sound of
birds here and there.

Carissa Dyer (13)

GONE!

Gone,
Death is forever
There is no going back.
Never again will I hear him talk
See him watching rugby
Never again will he call me 'Squeekers'.
It's like my heart is missing
Constantly I remember small forgotten things
He was and is my idol.
Talking with all his wisdom
I will never forget certain things.
The way he talked, never will I forget
He may be gone but I still love him.
He was and always will be,
My Pappie.

Elizabeth Polley (13)

THE SCHOOL TRUANT

How can I get out of school today?
I really don't want to go in,
The surf is thumping on the beach
With a hot and blinding sun,
How can I get out of school today?
I really don't want to go in,
There's a football match I'd like to see
With my favourite player in goal
How can I get out of school today?
I really don't want to go in,
I asked my dad and he said, 'No!'
'You are the teacher and have to go!'

Tom Bromfield (13)

THE NEW SPRING

Spring is a silvery spider's web,
shining and covered with dew.
Spring is a newborn baby,
walking on legs that are new.

Spring is a golden chick,
happy and running around.
Spring is a gentle shower,
cool and dampening the ground.

Spring is a trickling stream,
running on its bed.
Spring is a happy lamb,
skipping on ahead.

Spring is a cooling breeze,
gentle and fresh.
Spring is a sprouting seed,
brilliant and new.

Spring is an opening bud,
yellow and green.
Spring is a bright light,
as strong as a star.

Laura Waters (14)

BABIES

Babies are really annoying,
They cry so loud they pop your ear drums.
Babies are so smelly from their nappies.
Babies always ask you if you can read to them.
They spill food everywhere, getting it in their hair.
They wake up early in the morning.

Grace Jackson (11)

MY MUM AND DAD ARE ALIENS!

Both my parents are aliens,
So how do I stay on earth?
Am I just an exception?
Or was I swapped at birth?

Do they just do it to me?
Or does she always wear strange clothes?
But, I've always wondered why . . .
He put all his socks in rows.

Will I grow into one of them?
Please tell me it's not true.
I've grown up asking questions
But really, I'm just like you.

Emily Harvey (14)

THE HEROIC DEATH OF MANY POTATOES

I was ripped out of the ground,
Without making a sound.
I was taken far away,
I hoped just for the day.
I was taken to a place which wasn't a field,
Put in water, washed and peeled.
I was cut into slices
But not into dices.
Next thing I knew, I was being fried,
At this point I should have died
But I didn't and I lived to see,
Human teeth squashing me.

Thomas Le Vine (14)

MY MUM AND DAD ARE ALIENS

My mum and dad are hippies,
And wear all hippie clothes.
My dad has long hair,
And sandals with open toes.

My mum and dad like music,
From artists I don't know.
Ralph McTell, Cat Stevens,
And to their concerts they do go.

My mum and dad are oldies,
And talk of the good old days.
When electricity wasn't invented,
And the only entertainment were plays.

My mum and dad are aliens
And are really hard to tame.
They embarrass me completely,
But I love them all the same.

Helen Donovan (15)

MY MUM AND DAD ARE ALIENS

My mum and dad are very strange,
they often look into the sky.
They say they like the moon,
I sometimes wonder why.
They eat unusual foods,
and drink unusual drinks.
I asked them why they were so weird,
they looked straight into my eyes, and said . . .
We're aliens!

John Moore (14)

THE FREEDOM OF 1984

Freedom is slavery
Freedom is chance
Freedom is peace of mind
Freedom is choice.

Freedom is speech
Freedom is courage
Freedom is love
Freedom is to be whoever you want to be.

Freedom is Christian
Freedom is Jewish
Freedom is Muslim
Freedom is Coloured.

Freedom is the freedom to say $2 + 2 = 4$.

Gemma Curnow (14)

THE LITTLE LAKE

The little lake glistening and gleaming
Always seeming clear and blue,
The water and air always new,
The trees at the side rustling in the wind,
The leaves floating in the water,
Fish jump out,
And land with a big splash,
The rowing boats sit on the peaceful little lake,
Tied up to the pontoon
Ducks and swans flying over,
Quacking wherever they go,
The little lake is forever and ever.

John Woolcock (14)

If I Was Head Teacher

If I was head teacher,
My school would be,
A crazy place,
For you and for me.

School would be,
From ten until one.
All that free time,
For everyone.

Parties in the gym,
Food fights in the hall.
Teachers strung up in fishing nets,
Tortured until they fall.

PE would be cancelled,
Maths and English too.
Science, geography and history,
They would be banned too.

So you see my fellow pupils,
My school would be the best.
I'll be the leader of your leisure time,
So let's put it to the test.

Laura Packford (14)

Sharks

S wimming through the sea
H unting all the fishes for tea
A ggressive
R obust
K illing everything in sight
S neaking through the sea.

William Harvey (11)

MY MUM AND DAD ARE ALIENS

I'm sure my mum and dad are aliens,
though they assure me they are not.
I see them wearing hippie clothes,
I'm sure they've lost the plot.

I saw Mum on the stairs last night,
and I began to wail.
'Like my orange flares?' she said,
'Got them from a garage sale.'

My dad makes funny noises,
down in the garden shed.
Whirring, clashing, banging sounds,
he must be off his head.

My mum she is an odd case,
She's really, really weird.
The other day she was at the sink,
Bleaching out her beard.

They're so bizarre and strange,
I can't get it in my head.
Why can't they just act normal?
Can I have some others instead?

Verity Henderson (14)

MY PARENTS ARE ALIENS

Last night I saw through a crack in the door,
My dad unscrewing his head,
You'd think at this sight - I'd be throwing up all night,
Because, my dad should be dead,
But out popped a new one, only thing 'twas a blue one,
And the no more said.

But tonight at tea time,
When everyone felt fine,
My mum went up to bed,
I walked in through the door,
To see her head on the floor,
And the rest of her body in bed.

Ben Brosgall (15)

THE STORM

In the distance dark clouds forming,
Buzzards circle in the sky.
In the distance a storm building,
Animals hide in places dry.

A strong wind all around is blowing,
Trees begin to bend and sway,
A strong wind around the houses howling,
Sending people on their way.

Thunder rumbles, the sound foreboding,
Flowers shut their petals tight.
Thunder rumbles, the sound is deafening,
Sunlight fades to the dark of night.

A lightning flash, a baby screaming,
In mother's arms some comfort found.
A lightning flash so bright it's blinding,
Then quiet, silence all around.

Heavy raindrops on the ground are falling,
In the yard large puddles form.
Heavy raindrops on the window splashing,
Here I sit and watch the storm.

Daniel Torrie (13)

LIFE

Life is so strange,
How did it ever happen?
You start off as an egg,
Then you grown up to something else.
It may be weird,
But I'm glad it happens,
Otherwise I would never be here,
No one would.
I do wish school was left out,
Well we can't have it all right.
I do ask myself this though,
Why do we have to die?
We lose everything,
Friends, family, belongings,
Everything why?
It just goes like that.
So now I'm telling you,
Make the most of your life,
It's great while it lasts!

Charlotte Kent (13)

MY MUM AND DAD ARE ALIENS!

Yesterday I saw my mum's real face too horrible to describe,
But she claimed it was just a mud mask and offered me a bribe.
I said I'd keep my mouth shut anyway in case she zapped me with her
                                                            laser eyes,
Then ran into the dining room to tell Dad the great surprise,
But he looked up from behind his paper, I let out a scream,
But then I felt a nudge in my side and realised it was all a dream!
I got up to the window to look at all the stars,
Only to see my mother's ship on its way to *Mars!*

Kathryn Coyne (14)

MY MUM AND DAD ARE ALIENS

My mum and dad are aliens
or so it seems to me.
Walking is their hobby
But I'd rather watch TV.

My mum and dad are aliens
they tell me not to bet.
They listen to the radio
I'd rather surf the net.

My mum and dad are aliens
they're always reading books.
They tell me to tidy my room
and eat what Mum cooks.

My mum and dad are aliens
they send me to bed at nine.
I always make a scene
but I love them because they're mine.

Matthew Brown (13)

A TROUBLESOME CHALLENGE

From upstairs I heard Mum shout,
Matthew dear I must go out,
Amy needs to change her nappy,
Do it now and make her happy.
Mummy's left, we're all alone,
Never mind she'll soon be home.
Now I know what I must do,
Oh no, Amy, you've done a poo!
I don't know if I can cope,
Never mind, I live in hope.

Matthew Johns (13)

IF I WAS A HEAD TEACHER . . .

If I was a head teacher
I would bring back the cane,
this would stop brats from being a pain.

If I was a head teacher
I would be really mean,
and make sure that children
were healthy and clean.
They would all have good grammar
and play the guitar.
They would all play golf
and be under par

If I was a head teacher
I'd have strict staff,
just to make sure children
didn't laugh . . .

Aaron Ruffell (13)

IF I WERE HEAD TEACHER

If I were head teacher life would be great,
The pupils would be early, I would be late.

Bread and cheese for the pupils, five-star food for
me,
I would go on all the school trips, all for free.

I would set no homework, it's a pest to mark,
I would spend lunchtimes snoozing in the park.

If I were head teacher I would bring back the cane,
For the pupils *and* their parents who are such a
pain.

Stuart Trewhella (13)

IF I WERE HEAD TEACHER

If I were head teacher of our school
I wouldn't act the fool,
I would burn school uniform,
In a big room,
There would be shorter terms,
For money raising, teachers eating worms,
Days would be shorter,
Holidays longer,
With Sky TV in every room,
And trips to the moon,
I would build up phone bills,
And teach everyone football skills,
If I were head teacher of our school,
I wouldn't act the fool,
Or would I?

Joanne Pratt (13)

I DON'T SEE WHY

I don't see why we have to wear uniform,
I don't see why drama is just to perform.
I don't see why music consists of so much rhyme,
I don't see why at home our parents can't have permanent peacetime.
I don't see why I always have to have a pie,
I don't see why sometimes I have to lie.
I don't see why many people are scared of bats,
I don't see why there isn't a shop that sells rats.
I don't see why so many people cry,
I don't see why I have an itching eye.
All of these things could be changed . . .
. . . I just don't see why.

Stephen Hancock (13)

MY MUM AND DAD ARE ALIENS

My mum and dad are very strange,
All my friends think they're insane.
They always say these funny things
'Don't answer the phone just let it ring.'

'Don't be silly just be funny
then you will meet the Easter Bunny.'
'If you eat all your tea,
then you'll be big and strong just like me.'

'Eating your carrots can make you see in the dark.'
My mum and dad would take me down to the park.
When you are on the swings,
they would say these weird things.
'Do you think I have got eyes in the back of my head.'
Well I hope you enjoyed this poem you have just read!

Aimee Louise Holland (13)

MY MUM AND DAD ARE ALIENS

My mum and dad are aliens
They're not like me at all.
They always crawl
Even when I ask them to walk.
My mum and dad are aliens
I'm always wondering
What goes on in their minds.
Once they told me that they
Came from a planet unknown to my kind.
I wish they would go back there
But leave me behind.

Daniel Aylward (13)

WALK

Everywhere I go
Every step I know
I don't know where I am
I can't see a thing.

This mist surrounds me
Me and everything
The only thing I see
Are the eyes behind that tree.

I shout to my friend
There he is
He runs towards me.
I wonder why
He leaps in the air
Pins me to the floor
Licks my face,
Stop Fido!

Sean M Williams (13)

MY MUM AND DAD ARE ALIENS

My mum and dad are aliens
They have eyes in the back of their heads.
They tell me strange things and nag me
To tidy up my bed.
They always know what I'm doing
I can't get away with a thing.
All these small things are driving me totally crazy!
I am now convinced my mum and dad are aliens,
Never mind, I'm probably one too.

Adam Floyd (13)

WHY?

Why do the birds sing in the trees?
Why do we have little nobbles on our knees?
Why can we see things through our eyes?
Why do people get annoyed with sties?
Why do we cry when we are sad?
Why do we call our father Dad?
Why do we get embarrassed and go all red?
Why do we get tired and go to bed?
Why do we hurt when we fall down?
Why can't we breathe when we are drowned?
Why do we bleed when we get cut?
Why is a part of our body called a gut?
Why am I writing this poem called why?
I don't know why but some day I'll die!

Daniel Jarrett (13)

FIREWORK DISPLAYS!

Pop! Bang! Crash! Clang!
Say the fireworks as they explode in the sky.
Pop! Bang! Crash! Clang!
Squeal the screamers that soar up so high.
Most of the children cover their ears.
But I don't know what they have to fear,
It's only the fireworks clowning around.
With huge, big explosive ones and big bright Catherine wheels
And little sparkly ones that make a terrible squeal.
Some of the children like sparklers,
I do. I think they're great, but . . .
Fireworks aren't all fun and games,
You must also make sure that you're safe!

Amanda Barnes (13)

DEATH

He flies through the night in his jet-black cloak,
On his nightly rounds,
Riding high in the clouds on his magnificent horse,
The blade of his scythe,
Gleaming in the moonlight,
A menacing grin upon his face.
Around his waist hangs a timer,
The grains of sand falling,
Falling at an increasing rate.
Death's horse descends below the clouds
And comes to a halt near a lonely shack,
Death dismounts scythe and all,
He starts towards the rickety wall,
And he passes straight through it.
Alone in a bed lies an old man,
Wrinkled and stiff with age,
A few grains remain in the timer round Death's belt,
All he can do is offer a few words of comfort,
To the old man,
And as the last grain falls,
Down comes Death's scythe,
With one swift blow.
The old man passes over to the other side,
Death remounts his horse and takes to the sky
He doesn't want to be late for his next appointment.

Andrew Wright (13)

GARY

My little brother is a terror,
And always wants to fight.
He's always talking - he never shuts up,
Even in his sleep at night.

He's always watching Cartoon Network,
Or playing with his toys,
He always says that, 'Girls are wimps.'
And the world should be mainly boys.

He annoys me with his silly antics,
Or his passion for chocolate eclairs,
I chase him round and round the house,
Including up the stairs.

He's clever and really brainy,
And at school does really well.
I take this chance to tell my brother,
'Gary, I think you smell!'

Penny James (13)

THE VOLCANO

Uh-oh, Oh no! What have I done?
Now he's going purple, it's time to run
And now here it comes
Like a volcanic explosion
The room starts to shudder
His eyes like fire,
Was what I did really that dire?
His voice is booming,
He boxes the room in
I'm out of the door like a shot, with a slam.

Loveday Morris (15)

IF I WERE HEAD TEACHER

If I were head teacher of the school
I think it would be really cool
School meals would be a thing of the past
We'd all have McDonalds
What a blast!
There'd be no school uniform as that is
Uncool
Wear what you want
That would be my rule.

There'd be no homework
Just one rule to obey
Pupils must watch 'South Park' at least once a day
There'd be no prefects
Head Girl or Head Boy
Everyone would be equal
Oh what a joy!

Emma Stewart (15)

IF I WAS A HEAD TEACHER

If I was a head teacher,
I would get rid of the uniforms,
I would run a brilliant school,
The lunches would be yummy.
The lessons would be cool,
I would get rid of English and maths.
You could get to choose your lessons at only 3 lessons a day,
I would never give out detentions or internal
Suspension and never suspensions.
I would let the pupils leave at any time they like,
And I would make school fun for all to enjoy.
I wish I was the head teacher but I'm not.

Alison Charman (11)

MY MUM AND DAD ARE ALIENS!

My mum and dad are aliens,
It's scary but it's true.
I can prove it if you don't believe,
With evidence for you.
On searching through a scrap book,
I stumbled across something weird,
A woman with long hippy hair
And a strange man with a beard.
They were taller than expected,
With big platforms for their shoes,
A big fluffy ball of hair on his head,
And flares that accompanied too!
Under close examination,
I was horrified to see
That the couple in the photograph,
Were known to you and me.
My mum and dad are aliens,
It's scary but it's true.
Watch out for the eyes
In the backs of their heads,
As they might come after you!

Louise White (16)

IF I WERE HEAD TEACHER . . .

If I were head teacher of Mounts Bay School
I'd have a party every day or maybe a ball,
We'd have no books or work to do,
We'd groom our pets and feed them too.
We'd torment the teachers (like they do to us)
Give them IS and kick up a fuss.
There is no code of conduct, just one thing to obey,
And that is come to Mounts Bay and party every day!

Fiona Jarrett (16)

CATHERINE AND HEATHCLIFF

Out on the moors we wander,
Just me and my love - Heathcliff,
Nothing or no one else around,
Just our love to keep us warm
And light us a safe way home.
So free and so far,
We have come together,
He broke the chains that held me at the Heights,
He opened my mind and let my heart, body and soul loose,
He freed me in more ways than one,
He changed my life,
He turned me around,
He opened my eyes,
Now it's him, I finally realise.

Gemma Smith (16)

MY MUM AND DAD ARE ALIENS

My mum and dad are aliens,
They come from outer space,
And I am quite sure,
They're not part of the human race.

They walk around their room,
With huge boggly eyes,
And the normal people tell me
That my dad even flies.

They come into my room at night,
They look around what I call my base,
They just stand there and say,
'Look at the state of this place.'

Martin Oats (14)

I DON'T KNOW

Why are there so many surprises in the world
Why are there so many stories untold?

I don't know, I don't know.

Why does the sun shine only in the day
Why is that man not jolly and gay?

I don't know, I don't know.

Why don't the poor become the rich
Why do dogs always itch?

I don't know, I don't know.

Why do the stars stay up in the sky
Why is it pigs can't fly?

I don' know, I don't know
Why don't you know?

Steven Cheal (13)

HAMMY THE GREAT

My pet hamster is very good,
He can do almost anything,
Roll over, jump,
He is called Hammy the Great,
I haven't seen him today,
He is probably practising for his next big show,
He is very nosy,
He pokes his nose out to see what is going on,
His house is very neat and tidy.

Rebecca Nicholls (11)

My Dog Jessie

My dog Jessie is as funny as can be,
She eats almost anything,
including garden peas.

My gran and granpa across the yard love her too,
Granny gives her bits and scraps,
and Jessie won't let granpa tie up his shoe.

The neighbours feed her chocolate biscuits,
they're very naughty, aren't they?
How can I say that . . . as I do too!

*When night-time comes, she is let in
To lie by the Aga - be loved and go to sleep.*

Gemma Richards (11)

Autumn

Azure sky turns dark.
Billowing banks of mist come with a chill.
Whimpering wind arises, bringing fresh air.
Plants that lived, wither and die.
Grass is crisped, by the chilling wind,
Silvery, slimy trails left by snails.
Sweet English apples fall ripe and full-flavoured to eat.
Birds sing in melodious tunes.
New different aromas fill the air
Glowing fires warm and cheer the sky
The sun shrinks and dies.
Whilst leaves turn brown and the days mellow.

Chloe Redman (14)

MY MUM AND DAD ARE ALIENS

My mum and dad are aliens they say things like:
'I've got eyes in the back of my head,
Be good and the Easter bunny will bring you an egg,'
They do things like:
Sing nursery rhymes,
And send me to bed at unreasonable times,
They have sayings like:
'Watch too much TV and your eyes will go square,
Eat runner beans and you'll run like a hare,'
They make things up like:
Storks bring babies,
And that the tooth fairy takes your teeth.
My mum and dad really are aliens!

Robin Richards (13)

THE HOLE THROUGH TIME

This is a dark and foreboding place,
A beautiful calm world,
A world flowing through time.
For past eras,
There have been horrid torture techniques,
Gruesome guillotines and horrid hangings,
Yet some times are amazing,
The great Greeks and the perfect Persians,
All of time is different.

But it remains,
As time is never ending,
But man is.

Hector Roddan (11)

IF I WAS HEAD TEACHER

If I was head teacher
I would kill the preacher.
There wouldn't be any rules
But you'd better come to schools.
It would be all fun
And no homework by the ton.
School would start at eleven and end at three
With lots of food that's free.
The teachers would be taught
The kids would have sweets that they've bought.
Chewing gum would still be banned
A skate park built on spare land.
Computer consoles in along with all the games.
Clothes would have to be branded names
A bouncer at the door
To stop all you bores.
If you're late don't worry
I'll only make you sorry.
Overall you'll want to come to school
Because it's really cool!

Michael Oxley (13)

DON'T GO IN THE BASEMENT!

Don't go in the basement.
There's a monster who lives down there
He has big blue eyes and razor teeth
And green and purple hair.
Last week he ate my grandad,
He also ate my gran,
I'm definitely not going down there
He's scarier than the *bogeyman.*

Josh Stevens (12)

WHAT IF?

Last night while I lay thinking here,
Some what ifs crawled inside my ear,
And pranced and partied all night long,
And sang their same old what if song.

What if I forget my pencil case,
What if mouldy yellow spots grow on my face?
What if I miss the bus for school,
What if something explodes the hall?
What if I had a scare,
What if I lost all my hair?
What if I tripped over a shoe lace,
What if something wipes out all the human race?
What if I lost my eyesight,
What if there was no night?
What if I get run over,
What if I buy a Rover?
What if I walk into a tree,
What if I break my knee?
What if I had a pet snail,
What if I saw a quail?

Everything seems swell and then,
The night-time what ifs strike again.

Katherine Pascoe (11)

RED

Red means danger,
Like a mountain ranger,
It's the colour of the sun,
Gives you a lot of fun.

Flowers are red,
They make you stay in bed,
Passion and love,
As peaceful as a dove.

Elizabeth Dauncey

WHAT IF

Last night while I lay thinking here,
Some 'what ifs' crawled inside my ear.
They danced and partied all night long,
And sang the same old 'what if' song.
What if a monster was standing in the air,
What if I discovered I had no hair?
What if I found a £20 note,
What if I made an antidote?
What if I fell and broke my leg,
What if I swallowed a wooden peg?
What if I get angry and start to shout,
What if I let all my secrets out?
What if I get ill and then die,
What if I get upset and cry?
What if comedians stopped being funny,
What if the world was made of money?
What if my family suddenly died,
What if everyone starts to cry?
What if oranges had no orange peel,
What if we had a serious drought?
What if the 'what ifs' strike again?

Caroline Kliskey (11)

WINTER

Robins chirping to welcome winter,
Jack Frost out on his rounds,
Frostbitten fingers and toes,
Snowflakes falling down on the icy ground.

Heaters at full blast,
Fire glowing in the darkness,
Grandparents telling stories of the past,
Families meeting together.

Brightly coloured windows,
Christmas trees standing tall and proud,
Happy carollers in the distance,
By the fire toasting marshmallows.

Rosy cheeked children,
Happy holidaymakers,
Christmas lights gleaming in the mist,
A sly fox creeping around for food
Soon the cuckoo will be
Welcoming spring!

Victoria Goldsworthy (12)

MY SISTER IS AN ALIEN!

My sister is an alien,
She is blue and very hairy.
She sleeps under the bed,
And looks like she is dead.
She likes to eat her veg and
Jumps off the window ledge.

Hayley Richards (11)

IF I WAS A HEAD TEACHER

If I was a head teacher,
And I was in a bad mood,
I'd whip the children back and front,
And not give them any food.

I'd starve them all for months on end,
And if they started to scream and shout,
I'd break their arms and legs and toes,
And hope they'd never mend.

But if I was a head teacher,
And I was in a good mood,
I'd give them all the sweets and chocs,
So they could stuff themselves around the clock.

I'd give them lots of presents and toys,
And let them do what they like,
But seeing as I'm working with children,
I'd never be in a good mood so forget all those toys.

Emma Langthorne (11)

SLOSH

I soar across,
I'm down,
I drift along,
Around and down again,
He hits me with a blast,
I pick him up and tow him along,
I stop now and let him down,
I flow up on the grounded rock,
And soak in,
Then I flow back to hiding again.

James Charlesworth (11)

ARENA OF BUMPER CARS

A rena of doom
B ash them
C ripple them
D estroy your opponent
E veryone's your enemy
F righten them
G rab the steering wheel
H old on tight
I ndestructible is my car
J ack up your car for repairs
K ing of the ring
L ives at risk
M aim your enemy
N ever have been beaten, never will be
O verturn their vehicles
P ull apart their cars
Q uads are not allowed
R obust and tough cars
S peed addict
T otal destruction
U ltimate destruction zone
V alley of doom
W rite off their cars
X mas they won't have (they'll be dead)
Y ellow cars die!
Z oom off victorious.

Matthew Orchard (11)

MY LITTLE SISTER

My little 5 year old sister,
twists everything I say.
One day I didn't play with her,
and so she shouted I was mean to her!
My friends think she is cute,
with her pink dresses and ribbon bows.
They don't know the half when she
wakes me up at 5 in the morning,
hitting me with her Teletubby Po.
My little sister's toys are everywhere,
and I am usually late for school.
Once I ended up taking my sister's colouring book,
and as you can imagine, the teacher was not impressed,
when I turned up with a colouring book and failed my test.
My little sister is such a brat,
and only stays still when she's watching Art Attack.
Then she uses her creative mind to draw on anything she finds.
My little sister!

Kellie Thatcher (15)

ATTACK!

It shot up the stairs,
Approaching nearer and nearer,
With eyes glowing and teeth showing.
It growled and hissed,
Its legs thundered on the ground.
It proceeded; faster and faster,
Then it unsheathed its claws,
Preparing for the big pounce . . .

Jump! Thud! Scratch! Miaow!
The kitten had caught the feather!

Tom Potter (11)

I MET

One day as I walked down the road
I met a giant slimy toad.
I met a great big hairy spider
walking with a man who was not much wider.
I met a funny little pig
who with a big goose danced a jig.
I met a lovely dapple horse
walking in high heels of course.
I met an elephant, big and fat
who had a best friend, a little cat.
I met a dog who had a sore nose
with a little girl called Rose.
I met a monkey in a pair of shorts
and a family of hedgehogs with lots of snorts.
I met a kangaroo hopping along
and a nightingale singing a song.
I met a cow who came from Peru
who welcomed me with a high pitched moo.
I met a donkey who kicked at me
and also a goat whose name was Billy.
I met a rat who was rather nice
he's a teacher with a class of mice.
I met a gerbil small and brown
who had a great big golden crown.
I met a rhino with big long horns
who's swimming pool was full of prawns
and then I fell into a stream
and woke with a start, it was just a dream.

Nicola Davey (11)

MY HOUSE

The fire is like a roaring dragon.
The carpet's like a fluffy bear that never moves a muscle.
The TV is like my friend Adela that never stops talking.
In the kitchen the kettle shrieks.
The toaster spits out the toast like water coming out of a tap.
In the bathroom the shower claws the bath with its big wet claws.
The plughole swallows the water with its huge wide mouth.
In my bedroom is my kingdom.
Servants coming in and out taking orders from me.
My stereo is like a musician that never stops playing his trumpet.
My bed's like a soft cloud that stays in one place all the time.
My bike is like a prisoner that's crying 'Let me out of this hall.'

Kate Newby (11)

SWEETS

Sweets, sweets, sweets,
all I can eat is sweets.
A big juicy Twix,
or even a pick and mix.

Sitting in a chair guzzling them down,
pink, blue and also brown.
Eating sweets is a dream,
chocolate with cream.

A king size Mars,
or even shaped as cars.
But please give me sweets,
because all I can eat is sweets.

Cara Lea Moseley (11)

RYAN GIGGS

Ryan Giggs is the greatest footballer on earth
His fantastic skills stun his opponents
He soars down the wing
And flies past the defence
The goalie dives at his feet
But he rides the challenge
The goal gapes before him
He shoots with his favoured left foot
He scores!
Ryan Giggs scores for Manchester United
The crowd roar
The whistle goes
The match is over
United win 3-2
And it's all down to Ryan Giggs.

Peg Murray Evans (11)

RED

Red he said,
is fire and blood,
paint and glass,
there's red in our class!

Red she said,
is roses in bloom,
an apple on a tree,
the inside of a tomb!

We wear red clothes,
we have red lips,
we even have red paper clips!

Camilla Stephenson (11)

WINDOW

I sit and look out of my window,
Where I see a colourful rainbow,
A lady walked past wearing a red coat,
I see a man diving from his little boat,
There's another man fishing,
As the waves keep splashing,
A man walks past with a plate,
Looking at his watch for the date,
Playing in the river water,
Is a mother and daughter,
There's also some high rocks,
Standing on top is a man with white socks,
The lady comes back with her red coat,
The man comes in with his little boat,
The sun goes down,
There isn't a sound.

Vanessa Haines (11)

GREEN IS . . .

Green is the colour of Flubber,
Green is the colour of my rubber.
Green is the colour of snot,
Green is the colour of a green paint pot.
Green is the colour of tall green trees,
Green is the colour of little puny peas.
Green is the colour of a table top,
Green is the colour of an apple flavoured pop.
Green is the colour of my English book,
Green is the colour of the dinner cook.
        Green is my favourite colour.

Bryan Jenkin (12)

A SUMMER'S DAY

A summer's day in May
Is when I went out to play
My friend said 'Shall we go and see the clouds?'
She was called Jane
One of the clouds looked like a lane
My other friend came along then she was in a lot of pain
So we took her back to her mum and dad at home
By mistake we broke her dad's shaving foam
Her dad then started to moan
Because it was a hot summer's day we all had an ice-cream cone
When I got home my mum had been pricked by a thorn
My dad also played a terrible tune on a loud horn
That day also my new baby cousin was born
Then my brother arrived home from school, he was called Sean
And last before I went to bed I did a big yawn.

Adele Stevens (11)

COMPUTERS

Sitting down at the screen
all I can see is green.
The mouse is round
and makes no sound.
The keyboard is square
it's on the table there.
I like to play games
that I can win.
If I lose I get mad
they go in the bin.

James Stuart (11)

BURGLAR ABOUT!

Running through the shadows in the dead of night,
Pinching this, pinching that,
Quick let's *scat!*

Sprinting through the shadows when the moon is bright,
I'll have this, I'll have that,
Armed with my baseball bat.

Rushing through the shadows in the moon's bright light,
I'll take this, I'll take these,
I'm always on my toes.

I'm always very sneaky,
My name is Joe Whykeaky,
My occupation is *burglaring!*

Tom Somers (12)

SUMMER'S DAY

The golden sun throws its rays down onto the sea,
Making it sparkle silver like a diamond ring.
The fine sand seeps between your toes,
As you walk quickly not to get burnt.
Waves crash up against jagged rock statues,
And laps the shore stealing your footprints.
As the sun starts to set people leave,
All is quiet and a slight breeze picks up.
The bright shining stars come out one by one,
Like pearls scattered across the velvet sky.
The moon puts a silver streak onto the dark sea,
As all the animals camp under a dome of stars.

Megan Ruberry (13)

RECIPE FOR A NEW SCHOOL TERM

A scrumptious, delicious treat for a summer's day.
Mix together a posh pair of shiny shoes,
with a whisked up brand new jumper.
Slice and add a new maths book
then add a pinch of newly painted wall.
Blend in a pack of unchewed, neat, sharp pencils,
add a teaspoon of new, short hair styles.
Next pour in a slippery floor (nice to skid on),
knead in a shiny £1 W H Smith backpack,
and pour over melted, lonely, boring hall.
Sprinkle on top some freshly tarmaced playground
sticky from the sun.
'Pop' in four grumpy teachers.
Finally, bake it, until it rises and turns golden brown,
then place under the tree to cool . . .
'Then serve'.

Kathryn Waters (11)

MY PET FROG

I had a pet frog
Who lived under a log
He would jump and swim
And kick my friend Jim
My frog's name is Freddy
He's kicked my mum already
Which made her mad
And me sad
Because he went back to the pond today
Where he had to stay
Oh I wish he was here
So mum could see he is so dear.

Isabel Cattran (12)

WEIRD CREATURES

The creatures in this poem
You should be told about,
They really are very strange
Thin and tall, short and stout.

They perform strange antics
Communicate in grunts,
Some are quite old fashioned
Some go out to hunt.

Most of these weird beings
Drink a thing named 'beer',
It makes them very happy
Of this there is no fear.

They all like watching
Others kick the ball,
It gives them quite a thrill
I think it's called 'football'.

Some are horrid,
Some are lovely,
Some are stupid,
Most annoy me.

I think you've got my meaning
And I'm running out of lines,
Boys are these weird creatures
For whom I have no time!

Jowanna Conboye (15)

HOPE

She ran joyfully through the grass fields,
she picked some flowers for her mother.
She slept peacefully, in her bed thinking about her future,
and remembering all the good times.
She got fed up with her parents.
How she wished she was an adult.
She was a British girl.

She ran for her life through the vast mine fields.
She couldn't find any flowers for her mother's grave.
She lay restlessly on the hard ground worrying about a possible
future and trying not to remember all the bad times.
She longed for parents, though she wished she was a girl again.
She had hope; although her supply of it was running low.
She was a Bosnian girl, but she always had hope.

Ben Curnow (15)

HEAD TEACHER POEM

If I was a head teacher,
I'd give them a cane,
If I was a head teacher,
I'd be really cool,
If I was a head teacher,
I'd teach them there at school,
If I was a head teacher,
I'd make them eat gruel,
If I was a head teacher,
I'd make them say I'm cool,
If I was a head teacher,
Which I'll never be because
If I was I'd sit down and have a cup of tea.

Laura James (11)

MY PARENTS ARE ALIENS

My mum is an alien
and so is my dad
When they start to shout
they really go mad
If they shout too much
they end up green
It really is the funniest
thing you've ever seen.

My dog is an alien
and so is my sister
because on the end
of her finger she has a
really big blister.

They always do things
the wrong way round
so I have to put them right
and they give me a pound.

Daniel Lomas (11)

IF I WERE HEAD TEACHER

If I were head teacher,
I would be a fearful creature.
The staff I did not like I'd sack,
I'd also bring caning back.

Rules would be very strict in school,
I could enjoy being totally cruel.
Punishment being a regular feature,
In my life as a head teacher.

Nick Gregory (15)

THERE ARE ALIENS NEXT DOOR

There are aliens next door,
They're horrible I'm sure,
I hear them snorting at night,
In the moonlight.

It could be green with slime,
But it makes me sick
When I dine,
Their grunting and groaning is definitely
    Not mine!

It could be my parents
Making the noise,
But my parents care
Even though I tell them about the alien bear.

I went up the stairs
And I heard the noise there.
I opened a door
And there was . . .
    My brother!

Elisabeth Redman (11)

MY MUM AND DAD ARE ALIENS

My mum and dad are aliens they live upstairs on the wall,
There are no spiders in my house because they have eaten them all.
Then came from space in a jam jar fuelled only by Coca Cola,
They crash-landed in a compost heap and
All they had to eat was rotting vegetables.
They found me in a bush sat next to a family of slugs,
And all I used to do each day was eat the rotting spuds.

Sarah Bond (11)

HEAD TEACHER

If I was a head teacher I'd have loads and loads of power,
If I was a head teacher the kids would be working every hour.
If I was a head teacher I'd make them sweep the floor,
If I was a head teacher they'd polish my office door.
If I was a head teacher I'd feed them dead bats,
If I was a head teacher I'd infest the classrooms with big rats.
If I was a head teacher I'd whack them with the cane,
I'd whack them so hard they'd go flying down the lane.
If I was a head teacher I'd give them all detention,
Then they would give me their full attention.
A head teacher is something I'll never be
Because when I grow up I'll just me!

Laura Jewell (11)

IF I . . .

If I was a PE teacher I would be rather cruel,
I would make them all do 50 press-ups,
Then make them run a mile or two,
While I sat in my office enjoying my cup of tea,
Afterwards I would line them up for a shower,
Water steaming red and hot,
As soon as they got soapy,
I would turn the tap to cold.
I would make them late for their lessons,
Also late for lunch,
I am sure they all hate me!
And call me unpleasant names.
But I know my mum loves me and
I will always be the same.

Joshua Richards (11)

MY PARENTS ARE ALIENS!

When I'm all snuggled up tight,
My parents are having a party!
How are you meant to sleep in that racket?

In the morning:
My mum sucks up all the milk
And just leaves the cereal!
See how weird she is,
And my dad's even worse!
After my dad reads the newspaper,
His eyes go red with steam!
Do you know what my parents have for breakfast?
Frogs' legs cereal!
How disgusting!

And my sister is even worse . . .
She doesn't sleepwalk, *she flies!*
At school she does her work in, well, 2 seconds.
She's really embarrassing at school.

      I hope you feel sorry for me!
      My parents are aliens
      Are yours?

Maryanne Goldsworthy (11)

IF I WERE HEAD TEACHER

If I were head teacher,
School would be so fun,
No more teachers screeching,
And no more doing sums.

The uniforms would be cool,
The hours would be shorter,
The toilets wouldn't look like a pool,
And the teachers would be our porters.

Tom Burlton (15)

MY MUM AND DAD ARE ALIENS!

My mum and dad are aliens,
They eat food that makes me quiver.
They love brussel sprouts and cabbage,
Kidney, heart and liver!

My mum and dad are aliens,
You only have to hear
The total gibberish they speak sometimes
It really is quite queer!

My mum and dad are aliens,
They can appear out of thin air.
Just when you think the coast is clear,
They materialise, right there!

My mum and dad are aliens,
They have got eyes in the back of their heads
And they put them to good use alright,
Watching every step I tread!

My mum and dad are aliens,
You can only see,
They are not human beings,
Compared with you and me!

James Richards (15)

BLUE THINGS

Light shades
Dark shades
Any shade at all
Blue can be the sky, or
A shining glistening pool.

Blue flowers glitter
In the bright sunbeams, or
It can be a blue dog
Barking in your dreams.

Blue fish swimming
Through the blue sea
A blue door opens
When you turn a blue key.

A blue ball bounces
On a blue plate,
And a blue elephant
Walks through a blue gate.

Blue is what you feel
When you're lonely and sad,
When you go on holiday
And miss your mum and dad.

Blue nosed carol singers
Gather round a tree
Blue is my favourite colour
Blue is for me!

Ellen Louise Waghorn (11)

THERE ARE ALIENS LIVING NEXT DOOR!

There are aliens living next door,
I mean a few more than four.
I see them go so many times to the bog,
And I have to walk their dog.
They sleep on their head,
And act like they play dead.
They must come from Mars,
But they do have some cars.
I don't know what their names are,
But someone called the woman Dar.
I hear they support Spurs,
But 'hey' they are my neighbours!

Maree Smith (11)

MY PARENTS ARE ALIENS

My mum is an alien,
She is normally green,
But sometimes she is red,
When she shouts at me.

My dad is an alien,
He is always red,
I think he comes from Mars,
And hit my flaming bed.

My sister is an alien,
She is always blue,
She doesn't drink water,
But she does eat glue.

Ian Tucker (11)

DREAMLAND

Tramping down the drive,
Looking all around.
Suddenly behind me,
I hear a creepy sound.
I turn around and look,
But nothing can be seen.
I carry on walking,
It must have been a dream.
While I am walking,
I hear the noise again.
I have a look in the bushes,
But something makes me refrain.
Nothing can I see,
So what shall I do?
I carry on walking,
Then I hear a big 'Mooooooo.'
I feel so relieved,
It was only a cow.
It escaped from the farmer's field . . .
Somehow!

Emma McClure (11)

THE SWEET SHOP

The sweet shop is full of sweets,
They are pouring out the windows,
If you walk past the sweet shop after school
It will be full of delighted children,
There are sherbets, liquorice, dolly mixtures,
Every kind of sweet,
If you go in you come out with bags full
And spend all of your riches.

John Stevens (11)

IF I WERE HEAD TEACHER

If I were head teacher,
Things would be very different from before,
School would be thrilling and exciting,
Not a bore.

If I were head teacher,
I would change the way things were run,
Children would have privileges,
Homework would not be done.

If I were head teacher,
Teachers would be called by first names,
There will be no school uniform,
French may even be fun and games.

If I were head teacher,
Kids would look forward to school,
Holidays will be miserable,
No place for a fool.

Andrew Stevens (15)

IN A GRAIN OF SAND

In a grain of sand I see an autumn day,
Fire in the eyes of a single drop of rain.
The sun shining on a tear of a love song never heard,
Heaven resting on the curl of a golden rose.
I see a peach being cut with the devil's hands,
Angels dancing on the souls of forgotten lands.
The birds give voice to their sweet soft song,
Whilst the sands are waiting for when life is to become.

Georgina Yates (11)

FARAWAY

The stranger shifted slightly,
Drank in the surroundings.

Dark sky above
Pressing down, a mental weight.
A feeble sun, heaving clouds.
Storms will come, but first is the stifling heat
And colourlessness of the land.
The strange alien land.
Desolate, lonely, barren, bleak,
But strangely inviting.

A ruined castle above,
On top of the majestic cliffs
Glares down.

The stranger is uneasy,
In a composed way.

This ancient land,
Is the birthplace of magic,
Where good fights evil,
Merlin lives, and people speak in the old tongue.
But this place is empty,
The only sound is the angry waves,
Clawing at the battered shingle.
Mystery envelopes the land like a cloak.

The landscape is physically scarred;
Several miles away is a forest,
Where the ground is swampy.
The sound of a fiddle,
Drifts on the wind,
And the stranger starts up the path
To follow the enticing tune.

Emily Wilson (14)

IF I WERE A HEAD TEACHER

If I were a head teacher
I wouldn't be a horrid creature.

No uniform each day
Things would always go my way.

If I were a head teacher
I wouldn't be a horrid creature.

No exams or other tests
Leave the classrooms in a mess.

If I were a head teacher
I wouldn't be a horrid creature.

Come to school twice a week
No homework for you to seek.

If I were a head teacher
I wouldn't be a horrid creature.

Helen Richards (13)

IF I WERE HEAD . . .

If I were head I would not be sitting here wondering what to write.
If I were head I would be out with my mates right now.
If I were head I would be able to stay up late
and have a lie in tomorrow.
If I were head I would not be flitting through the thesaurus
looking for words to impress the teacher with.
If I were head this poem would not have been written.

Kerry Knowles (15)

UNTITLED

There are aliens living next door,
they sleep on the kitchen floor.
They come from the planet Zog,
and have their dinner in the bog.
They look like gorillas,
arms and legs like caterpillars.
Their heads are like snot,
they go poo in a pot.
Their parents look like dogs,
and their relatives are just frogs.
Slime in their ears,
yellow and green soggy tears.
Their lion is tame,
I beat it and don't get the blame,
and my parents and them,
well they're just the same.

Clifford Morgan (11)

THERE ARE ALIENS LIVING NEXT DOOR!

I wake up at night hearing sound in my dream,
The whirring and hissing of steam.
I think there are aliens from Uranus and Mars,
They serve green slop and drink from shining jars.
They travel two hundred light years,
To come to a place where you have too many fears.
They stay in all day and come out at night,
These strange people fear the light.
These are the beings living next to me,
They're an odd sight to see.
I do hope they're many more,
Who want aliens living next door.

Kenneth Knight (11)

ALIEN

As I was walking home from school
I saw a very weird ghoul
Where had it come from? Why was it here?
I had to think fast, put my brain in gear.

When I got home I found a big bowl
What was this big thing? I just didn't know.
It looked like a spaceship, but I wasn't sure,
I studied it closely, I looked at the door.

I screamed and shouted with my surprise
My parents were green and had big eyes.

Now I have to live knowing I could be one too
Oh no, I'm turning blue!
I'm now an alien, like my mum
And now I'm feeling really glum.

Holly Hobson (12)

BLUE IS

Blue is the colour of the water
Blue is the water that goes down rivers
Blue is the colour of the blue whale
Blue is a smashing colour
Blue is sensational
Blue is electric blue
Pale blue
Dark, moody blue
When feeling blue.

Oliver Pridham (11)

My Cats

C ustard is my cat.
Yo U would love him if you saw him
S o sweet!
Some T imes!
A ttack cat
Fo R ever sweet!
D opey when he's sleepy.

A nd . . .
Do N 't forget his brother
He's calle D Willow.

W illow is my brother's cat,
I rresistible
We'l L love him for ever
L ovely!
L O vely (again!)
W illow is my brother's cat.

Jessica Lloyd (12)

If I Were Head Teacher

If I were head teacher, I would bring back flogging,
And make those vicious little kids go out jogging.
If I were head teacher, I would use a cane as my weapon,
To bring those naughty little brats out of a rebellious disposition.
If I were head teacher, I would have a luxurious, dark old study,
But those pathetic little excuses will be scurrying around worried.
If I were head teacher, my hours would be from nine till eleven,
But for those irritating little things, theirs will be from seven to seven.
If I were head teacher, my staff would be as fierce as tigers,
And would not go easy on the annoying little blighters.

Simon Jacoby (16)

IF I WERE HEADMASTER

If I were headmaster,
There would be disaster.

If kids mucked about,
I'd let the Rottweilers out.
Instead of detention,
I'd make them pay for my pension.
I'd enforce child labour,
As a money saver.
To build my office swimming pool,
Now *I'm* in charge of the school.

If I were headmaster,
There'd be no more laughter.

Michael Christopher Marten (15)

IF I WERE HEAD TEACHER

If I were head teacher
I would be nice and kind
The kids could do whatever they wanted
I wouldn't mind
Schooldays would be short
And holidays long.
Whatever they did it wouldn't be wrong
They could do whatever they chose
And on every sports day no one would lose
My school would be a place you
Wouldn't want to leave
And a place where everyone would achieve.

Donna Keeler (15)

STAR STRUCK

There's always hope in the blackest of night,
Always one star emitting its light.
It's a fresh promise things'll work out alright,
Even though darkness is presenting a fight.
That one speck of luminance brings us all hope,
Showing us life is too short to mope.
That sparkle of stardust leads us to cope
Just one tiny spot on my telescope.
It could be a planet, a world that is new,
Or a cluster of moons, a nova or two.
The constellations might scatter my view,
But still that lone star reminds me of you.

Inspired I find, by the night sky,
I choose to sit and ask myself why.
We are a galaxy, just you and I,
Who shine with excitement without needing to try.
We are like Gemini eternally bound,
Take a glance up and together we're found.
Always as one, stood hand in hand,
As we face boldly the Milky Way band.
But morning will come, you appear to forget
And I realise we will face problems yet.
Some more severe than we've ever met
But they will be solved with the birth of sunset.

Some say promise is born with the light
But given the choice I'd always choose night.

Jasmine Venning (15)

IF I WAS HEAD FOR THE DAY . . .

If I was head for the day,
I would make things my way.

No big tests,
Now that would be best.

Chewing gum wouldn't be banned,
Now that would be grand.

I would have my own personal slaves,
To play my part on the claves.

We would start late
That would be great.

Finish at three
To go home for tea.

We would ride our bike,
And wear whatever we like.

We would play music in class,
Loud enough to break the glass.

We would treat the teachers like they treat us,
Make them catch the bus.

Now that would be the best dream,
It would be better than eating ice-cream.

Lauren Richards (13)

IF I WERE HEAD TEACHER

Things would change if I were boss,
Things would shape up then,
If I were head, it must be said,
I'd ban all blue/black pens.

I think in fact I'd ban all pens,
And burn them at a stake,
'Coz pens are evil and mine blots,
And leaves a big ink lake.

Thinking on further than that,
Uniforms would go too,
I'd change it to whatever colour,
Just not white, black or blue.

School would be a party,
Lessons would be fun,
Conducted in the open air,
On grass and in the sun.

Being head could be such fun,
Could bring folk so much joy,
But I am just left dreaming,
A simple young school boy.

James Harris (13)

I FOUND OUT MY DAD IS AN ALIEN

I found out my dad is an alien,
It did not come as a surprise,
He always had pale skin,
Or even bright red eyes.

He would waddle to the kitchen,
And would hobble up the stairs,
But then again it's okay,
I really don't care.

Aran Jackson (12)

WHAT IF?

Last night, while I lay thinking here,
Some *What Ifs* crawled into my ear,
And pranced and partied all night long,
And sang their same *What If* song.

What if I wake up late?
What if I get bitten by a snake?
What if my hand gets stuck in the door?
What if I fall right through the floor?
What if I fall off the beam?
What if someone pushes me into a stream?
What if a tree falls on me?
What if I float out to sea?
What if there's poison in my cup?
What if I never wake up?
What if an alien landed in my backyard?
What if I turn into a bag of lard?
What if I get run over by a car?
What if then I become a star?
What if I catch a mink?
What would Mum and Dad think?

Everything seems swell, and then,
The night-time *What Ifs* strike again!

Debbie Lancaster (11)

I Discovered I Was An Alien

The girls at school call me an alien,
I think it's quite cool,
I don't know where I came from,
I think aliens always rule.

I've seen the movies, I've seen them all,
And UFOs are so cool,
I really like drinking blood,
I'm different in school.

I love being odd I eat bananas whole,
I wish I was an alien,
I'm used to being away from home
And I'm known as Nathan O.

Nathan John Oliver (11)

My Mum And Dad Are Aliens

My mum is green and slimy
My dad is purple and wet
My mum eats spiders and worms
My dad eats egg yolk and the rest
My mum sleeps on the floor
My dad sleeps under the carpet
My mum has four eyes
My dad only has three
Dad says 'A man cut it off in the army'
My dad has five tongues
My mum only has three
They are awfully different
But they act the same.

Mark Hosking (12)

My Mum And Dad Are Aliens

My mum and dad are aliens
They're from the planet Stress
Whenever I am naughty they flip into a mess
I know they don't mean to
But it puts me in a fest
They always want the last word
They even speak to lemon curd
To get their precious last word.
My mum and dad are aliens
They're from the planet Stress
My dad has seven eyes
And my mum's face looks a mess.
My mum and dad are aliens
They're from the planet Stress.

Luke Howes (11)

If I Were A President

If I were a president I would have lots of money,
And everything would be funny.
I would live in a big house
Not one as small as a mouse.
Smaller than the hall
But bigger than a swimming pool
And just in case you want to come
There will be guard dogs on the run
And just in case you don't believe me
Why don't you come and see me.

Ashley Jephson (12)

I Discovered I Was An Alien

When I discovered I was an alien,
I happened to be taking a bath,
all my body turned green,
but all I could do was laugh!

I wonder what my mum will think,
with me being slimy and green.
She'll probably put me in the garden
so I'll turn into a bean!

When I discovered I was an alien,
I still looked perfectly well,
I just won't take a bath any longer or,
I won't be very well!

Lauren Henderson (12)

Is Winter Coming?

Birds rushing towards the south,
Winter must be coming,
Humans rushing through the shops,
Winter must be coming,
Hedgehogs starting to hibernate,
Winter must be coming,
Otters building their winter dens,
Winter must be coming,
Small snowflakes floating down,
Winter is here!

Mark Clay (12)

A SCHOOLGIRL CRUSH

I can see you,
You're standing by Scott.
You're really cute,
And you're major hot!

You make me laugh,
When you snigger and joke,
I'd fancy you,
Even if you were flat broke!

Another four years,
And yet to come.
Can we go out together?
You're number one!

I miss you loads,
When you're absent from school.
I like you loads,
Even though you act like a fool!

I'll love you forever,
And for evermore.
It's you that I love,
It's you I adore!

I wish you could know,
You're really sweet.
When I go up to heaven,
I hope it's you that I meet!

Fenny Potts (11)

ME AND MY PONY

Me and my pony are really good
Did I know that I was you
What if he saw me?
What if I saw him?
Me and my pony are really sneaky
He gives me cuddles, I give him cuddles
What if I fell off?
What if he ran away?
Me and my pony are really happy
He can be so funny.
What if he came to me and kicked me?
What if I went to groom him and he wasn't there?
Me and my pony are really good and
I want to be with him forever.

Sara Graham (11)

MRS PAYNE

Mrs Payne comes from Teacher Stress Land,
But she's willing to lend a hand.
At night she gives her teacher friends a fright,
With an enormous bite.
I did not think you knew this,
But she can also start to hiss.
Miss wears a long green cape,
As her friends try to escape.
She walks down the street,
Like a normal person in the heat.
But deep down inside,
She's a monster - no one can hide.

Natasha Kearey (11)

My School Day

Off to school,
As a rule,
My new bag,
I must not drag,
In the rain,
It's such a pain,
For I am soakin',
Must take my coat in,
Hang on my peg,
My auntie said,
I'll do some reading,
Better than weeding,
Perhaps some sums,
Umm! Umm!
Now for a play,
That breaks the day,
And some lunch,
Munch! Munch!
Back to my desk,
For my first test,
I hope I passed,
I don't want to be last.

Mahala Martin (12)

If I Was A Head Teacher

If I was a head teacher, I would have teachers that never told you off.
If I was a head teacher, the seats would be very soft.
If I was a head teacher, I would throw parties every day.
If I was a head teacher, you'd have to pay.
If I was a head teacher, I would paint the school fluorescent green.
If I was a head teacher, sometimes I could be really mean.

Sarah-Jane Kewn (11)

I Like, I Hate

I like chocolate,
I like peas,
I like cornflakes,
They're very good for me.

I hate All Bran,
I hate nuts,
I hate papaya,
It gives you bad guts.

I like Coke,
I like Sprite,
I like milk,
But don't drink it at night.

I hate cherryade,
I hate squash,
I hate orange juice
It gives you a moustache.

I like Adidas,
I like Nike,
I like Reebok,
You need boots to go for a hike.

I hate pink,
I hate black,
I hate white,
But you can always take them back.

I like yellow,
I like red,
I like orange,
They're the colours of my bed.

Everyone knows my name
Apart from Mrs Payne.

Bryony Davidson (11)

MY PARENTS ARE ALIENS

When I went to bed
One night, I heard
A creak downstairs,
'Who is it, who is it?'
I cried. There was
No reply.
I sat in my bed and
Looked around the room,
Then bursting through
The door they came
With green skin and
Big brown eyes,
'Who are you?' I said aloud
'We are your parents.' they said.
They grabbed me by the
Arms and legs,
And took me outside,
We climbed into the
Spaceship and zoomed
Off to the moon.
Now I'm living on
Bread and cheese.
I hope we get
Back soon!

Casvelyn James (11)

If I Were The Headmaster!

If I were the headmaster
I'd show those little terrors who's boss.
If they misbehaved, it's their loss.
Nobody would mess with me,
Because I can assure you I wouldn't be happy.
If you speculated someone looking half dead
Then you definitely know they've been to see the *head!*
If I were headmaster
Slate and chalk would return,
That's right! They would soon learn.
The good old fashioned cane,
If struck with it, they'd feel pain.
So you'd better watch your step, Son
Or I'll soon make you run . . . !

Clare Laity (13)

I Am Not An Idiot

I am not an idiot,
Running into space,
Trying to eat the moon,
And getting it in my face,
Creating a big spoon.

I am not an idiot,
Banging my face,
Nosing into bags,
Crawling the human race,
Pretending to be a hag.

I told you
I am not an idiot!

Lucy Stubbings (11)

WINTER

My wellingtons sink in the soft smooth snow,
Making giant footprints wherever we go,
My breath heavily marked on the windowpane,
Little infants playing traditional snowball game.
Long spiky icicles hang full of hatred,
Piercing the air like daggers.

Warm mittens and long woollen scarves,
Hot cocoa in front of the fire and lots of laughs
Brittle ice protecting the lake,
From uninvited guests leading a path of fate,
Evenings get darker, colder, and dim,
Frost from the outside . . . mustn't let it in!

Home-made sledges zoom down the hills.
Children screaming, their faces full of thrills.
Snowmen densely spread out all over the place,
Always looking happy, with a carrot for a nose,
And mouldy turnip eyes
Their faces all innocent, never one to tell lies.

Smoke from the chimneys, puffing and chugging,
The fires blazing, spitting keeps us nice and snug.
The occasional flock of birds flies across the skies,
Interrupting the silence of the cool and unlit evenings
The snow starts to melt just like a magic trick,
All revealed is green lush grass, quite short but thick,
Little buds gasping for air.

Spring is on its way.

Charlotte Louise Lodey (13)

My Brother Is An Alien...

My brother is an alien,
Oh what can I do?
My brother is an alien,
One minute he's green, the next he's blue.
My brother is an alien,
He always gives me a fright.
My brother is an alien,
He makes me turn white.
My brother is an alien . . .

My brother is an alien,
Oh what can I do?
My brother is an alien,
What shall I do?
My brother is an alien,
But he smells like you,
My brother is an alien . . .
What can I do.

Natalie Boyns (15)

I Love Chocolate

C   hocolate I love it
H   eavenly taste
O   verpowering
C   uriously easy to eat
O   ut of this world
L   uscious
A   musement
T   asteful
E   asy-going.

Alison Pring (11)

In My Head . . .

In my head I think of . . .
What day it is.
What the day's going to be like.
What is going to be on the television tonight!

In my head I think of . . .
How my animals are.
What they are doing.
Do they miss me when I'm at school?
I just wonder!

In my head I think of . . .
What to write.
What new book to read.
What the teacher's saying.
In my head . . . I think this poem has got to end!

Toni Spurrier (13)

My Mum And Dad Are Aliens

My mum and dad are aliens
I found out the other night
When they unzipped their disguises
And it gave me quite a fright
Never come into my house again
Because you never know
You might turn into one of them
My mum and dad are aliens
My mum is black and blue
My dad is green and slimy
And that is very true.

Samantha Lowes (11)

IF I WERE HEAD TEACHER

If I were head teacher,
I wouldn't make ya
eat school dinners
full of cows' livers.

Although I would make you learn,
as part of the National Curriculum,
school wouldn't be so boring
if I were head teacher.

School uniform would be out,
scruffy blazer and torn tie,
you could wear anything
as long as you still say, 'Hi!'

This is what school would be like,
cool and not boring,
you wouldn't be snoring
if I were head teacher.

Tracy Attridge (13)

LITTLE FROG

Small fat frog,
jumping in a muddy bog,
camouflaged always in the leaves,
swimming around in the autumn breeze.

Frogs are as slimy as green seaweed,
Bumpy body rubbing against the weed,
Slimy frog in my hand,
He hopped away and cannot be found.

Neil Mainwaring (12)

FLYING TO THE SUN

The sun I think is a great big light
I tried to figure out how it should light.
Then as soon as I found out why
I figured out why I could fly.
I flew here, I flew there,
I tried to fly up in the air.
I soon found out that I could fly,
I went right up in the sky,
So I decided that I would fly
To maybe the sun,
Yes maybe the sun.

So the next day I flew to the sun,
'Yes to the sun,' I said, 'yes to the sun.'
When I got there
Yes to the sun,
I was flying near the sun
Amongst the golden lashes of the next dawn.
Then it started to set at noon
And I had not lost my flying power yet.
Then I heard a clink and a clonk
And I found myself falling
Yes falling to the ground
I fell some more, I got my coat
And drifted past the sunset's last look.

Laura Jackson (13)

MY MUM AND DAD ARE ALIENS!

My mum and dad are aliens
well at least that's what I think.
I've never noticed this before
Their eyes don't even blink . . .

My mum and dad are aliens
you should see the way they walk.
Their feet are angled outwards
Their teeth are made of chalk . . .

My mum and dad are aliens
they never take a bath.
Their English is appalling.
They rarely even laugh . . .

My mum and dad are aliens
five sugars in their tea.
Their faces go a loomy green.
When they're too angry . . .

My mum and dad are aliens
I think you all agree.
The best thing for me to do.
Is to leave this family . . .

Lewis Barr (13)

TREES

Some trees are big,
Some trees are small,
But my tree is the best of all
I built a house big and strong
Where is everyone?
They must have all gone.
Now they won't see the very best tree.

I wake up next morning
Everyone's out,
Now what about?
Yes I will I'll show them the best tree of all,
But where has it gone?
I can't see the very best tree.

Sally Georgina Titus (12)

MY MUM IS AN ALIEN!

I noticed it first after school one day.
My mum was up the stairs
Lying in her bed, she was
Hugging her teddy bears.

She didn't look ill at all,
But she said she had the flu.
I knew there was something funny going on
Oh! What was I to do?

That night I crept down the hall,
Along to my mum's room.
I creaked open the door
And as quick as a flash
I heard a great big *boom!*

It came from outside, I was sure,
But noticed she was gone.
So now I knew that something was
Definitely wrong!

I looked outside, but had nothing to see
If my mum was an alien!

Then could I be . . . ?

Jade Jenkins (13)

IF I WAS HEAD TEACHER . . .

If I was head teacher
I'd dress up in cool clothes,
Have a wacky hairstyle
And even paint my toes.

I'd decorate the staffroom
In fluorescent tones,
Throw a massive party
Give the pupils mobile phones.

If I was head teacher
I'd drive a fancy car,
Install an escalator
And employ a singing star.

I'd build a huge jacuzzi
Get a swimming pool,
And after summer holidays
We'd enjoy going back to school!

Sophie Richards (13)

THE SEA

Blues and greens mixed together
full of life deep below waves
crashing and splashing at bottoms of cliffs,
such strong storms at sea.
Only few boats survive
The winds envelop the boats
then toss them in the air
and bashes them down into a watery grave.
The sea can be so calm then be so violent.

Kane Whitley (12)

WINTER

The biting wind cuts through the crystal sky.
Birds migrate to warmer climes.
Days die like yesterday's fire.
Dew shimmers on the pale grass.
Winter is coming.

The robin chirps in the frosted trees.
The crisp air wakes all living things.
The glowing sun slowly departs behind gloomy clouds.
Winter is upon us.

Slowly sun makes its presence felt once more.
The sky full with flocks of birds.
Days lengthen like the blossoming flower
Grass retains its luscious shine
Winter is going . . .

Josh Harris (14)

THE SUN

The sun our friend, our heat, our light,
The sun protecting us with its might,
The sun a glimmering ball of power,
Shining down upon us hour after hour,
But even the sun needs a break,
A space that someone else must take.
Father moon takes over at night,
Bathing us in his softer light,
Watching over us while we sleep,
Not a sound, not a peep.

Lasalle Simon (12)

WINTER

Winter has a cold heart, and cares for few.
It seems sad and unhappy,
But has no reason for this.
It has no sense of humour,
And co-operates with neither plant nor animal.
It's a pessimist, never looking to the bright
side of any situation.
An old man, with a bare, dead personality,
As if hibernating eternally.
Life was long ago drained from his dead body
leaving him hollow.
But he still comes around every year,
never experiencing anything in a different way.
He has to live his dull life again and again,
never dying, but never being reborn into
another season.

Daniel Williams (13)

I AM AN ALIEN

I am an alien from out of space
I walk around with a smile on my face.
My smile is so big, my face disappears
then all you can see is my wapping big ears!
Then when I sneeze my eyes pop out
and all you can hear are people that shout.
My feet are so sticky they stick to the ground
and all you can hear is this slodgy sound.
My legs are too short, my arms they are long
I also have this very long tongue.
I don't know why they run from me
Because I am only . . . two foot three!

Claire Graham (15)

NOTHINGNESS!

There is no life way up there.
No prince, no princess, no children so fair.
It's a place where not many people go
No Safeways, no Pioneer, no Tescos!

No beaches, no sand - only dried up sea
No sign of leaves, plants or trees!

No horses, no ponies
No old fogies!

No cars, no motorbikes
No day nor nights.

So when you think your life's in a mess
Look up there and think of . . . the nothingness!

Morwenna Matthews (12)

WITHOUT YOU!

Without you, I would not want to wake up in the morning.
Without you, I don't know how I could talk to anyone
Without you, I would see no point in life.
Without you, I have nothing to dream about.
Without you, I'd have no one to depend upon for comfort.
Without you, I would always be alone.
Without you in my life . . . I would not want to live.
Without you in my heart . . . I would sink down
Without you . . . !

Patricia Gee (15)

LOVE LETTERS

Staring at a blank page
Not knowing what to write.
Wishing there was a way
To end my plight.
Hoping every day, hoping every way
Wishing for the words,
I long for him to say
How can you lay your feelings on paper
When you're not quite sure.
If your so-called emotions
Are really yours at all.
Composing a love letter
Isn't that much better.
Than keeping your feelings inside
Where your love for him you hide.

Lucy Burgan (13)

STAR

No light, no air, no life, all bare!
It has no light of its own
But someone else's!
It has no name of its own
But the same
As each and everyone amongst it . . .

Jess Croucher (13)

SURFING

Surfing is the best sport,
it's like a thrill from the bill and
still to this day I get a thrill.
Surfing is not just a piece of fibreglass.
It is hard so - no wimps allowed!
I like it when you are on the lump
and you get a bit of a stomach bump
and a bit of a rummy tum tump.
So as you can gather it's a bit of fun
Don't sit in on a hot day -
come down to Gwenva and
have a bit of a play!
Oh no! I have just been dumped by the sea
that will teach me till tea off I be!

Laurens Everitt (11)

THE REGAL GOLDEN EAGLE

He wears a crown on his head as he soars through the air.
Never makes a mistake and always takes care.
All the hares look up to him in the sky,
Looking out for talons, razor sharp - as he flies.
He's got a large beak to match his wingspan.
And never changes his attacking plan.
He swoops down low, just above the ground.
Talons out - takes 'em down!
Quick, darty, big and fast
And is regarded highly . . . as king of the woodland!

Zach James Wooley (12)

MY CAT

My cat Tigger, loves fighting
With my next door neighbours cat.
He's always clawing and biting
But he always sleeps on my bedroom mat.

My cat Tigger is really sweet,
Even though my mum hates him.
My cat's the coolest in the street,
But there's trouble when he sees Tim.

Tim jumps and scratches
Tigger runs and jumps.
They roll down the street with hate,
hair gets ripped out
then I start to shout
'Will Tigger ever get a mate!'

Sandra Good (13)

THE STAR WITH NO NAME

No name to call its own - yet!
The ball of burning gas
shines its little light
to guide the earthlings safely home
at night . . .

Untouched, uninhabited.
The star is a silhouette in the darkness.
No day . . . no night
just a constant burning light.

Maria Eddy (12)

MY MUM AND DAD ARE ALIENS!

My mum and dad are aliens.
They do the strangest things.
Light the fire in summer
They put the milk in the freezer,
My mum is the strangest
She washes my PE kit
When it isn't even smelly.
She goes to school to teach
The children in her class are like zombies.
Wandering in and out.
No wonder they say she is from another
Planet - because she is!
My dad is really weird
He talks end on end about nothing.
I hope I have proven that
My mum and dad are aliens,
Hey! beam me up Scottie!

Jonathan Pollard (11)

FOOTBALL

Football is a great game for some, but not for others.
Football - some get hurt, but not others.
Football is tiring for some, but not for others.
Football is about winning for some, but not for others.
Football is muddy for some, but not for others.
Football is about scoring for some, but not for others.
Football is about celebrations for some, but not for others.
Oh yes! Winning is for some - but not for others!

Antony Vallance (12)

SNOW

Gently falling
soft and cool.
Winter calling
the frozen pool.

Morning has broken
a white blanket has come.
The freeze has woken
time for the tea and rum.

As cold as ice-cream
almost as good to eat.
A sleigh ride dream
swept off my feet.

Drifting flakes
Jack Frost too.
Spades, forks and rakes
Oh! What a do!

Children playing
having fun.
Snowman or something?
Until the sun.

James Stell (11)

NOTHING

Empty, no air, no people - nothing!
Never will a bird sit
It has no life on it
For life it is not fit
A deadness, a stillness
Nothing more . . . nothing less!

Lisa Olds (12)

THERE IS LIFE ON THE MOON!

There is life on the moon
but don't believe all those cartoons!

Aliens maybe
but no animals roam free.

No trees, grass or flowers grow
No rivers or streams flow.

All of these things are not up there
do you think that this is fair?

There is life on the moon
a human has been up there
and there's going to be another one soon!

Kelly Matthews (12)

MOON LIFE

There used to be three of us.
Me - you - and *him!*
We stood together on this moon - so dim
Him went away and didn't come back soon
I tried to follow *him*, but didn't get past Neptune!

We sent *him* a card saying 'Come back soon!'
I suppose *he* didn't get it, or *he* couldn't find the moon!

So now, there's just the two of us
Me and you . . .
If we didn't live on the moon, we wouldn't be talking to you!

Lydia Williams (12)

IF I WAS HEADMASTER

Merit, merit, merit.
Credit, credit, credit.
Cricket every day!

Bigger better portions.
Dinner-time is here.
Pasta, pasta, pasta.
I'm the headmaster.
If you want a break - take a break
But cricket every day!
The teacher's smiling
The pupils are smiling
Cricket every day!

Oh! The day goes faster
Now that I'm headmaster . . . !

Jeremy Kent (12)

NOTHING BUT SILENCE . . .

There's nothing there.
Up! Up high.
All you see is deep blue sky.
Floating planets all alone,
You wouldn't see a telephone.
No shops, no cops
No animals or robots.
Just silent sound
Of no one around.
In the nothingness of space . . . !

Jennifer Gee (12)

THE MOON PEOPLE ARE WEIRD

The people on the moon are weird,
They've all got a really long beard,
When they are going to school,
They roll up in a hairy brown ball.

The people on the moon are very strange,
They all live on a large mountain range,
And when there is an avalanche,
There's nothing left but a branch.

The people on the moon are half-dead,
Their brains are made of lead,
When you ask them for directions,
They don't even know what you've said.

I'm glad I'm not one of those people,
Because I would do all the stuff instead.

Martin Packford (12)

WHAT COULD LIVE ON THE MOON?

What could live on the moon?
Except for the rock or two
Maybe bright lights
That's how it's so bright
Maybe silver foil
That's why it's like dirty oil
Maybe the moon isn't made of rock
What is the moon?

Natasha Coates (12)

GROWING UP

Poked, prodded
sprinkled with water.
Dazzle, blinded
as it emerges on its journey.
Fully grown
tossing, swaying,
rocking gently in the soft wind.
Down falls its summer coat.
Crispy, crunchy
extremely warm for little animals.
New growth reaching
out to touch the sun.
Looks so splendid
in golds
and
greens.

Lisa Tunney (11)

SPACE-WALKING ON THE MOON

Space-walking; it's easy to do.
Anyone can do it - even you!
The spacesuit it tends to sway
From side to side - it orbits away.
It feels so weird in slow motion
But when you see everyone else - what a commotion.
There's nothing to stop you from flying off the moon.
So get *down to earth* you silly buffoon!

Darren Jones (12)

THERE IS SOMEONE UP THERE!

There is a lunatic living on the moon
he might be coming down here soon.

There is no light up there
he doesn't really care.

It is quite round
he doesn't stand on the ground.

He floats in the air
like a big wheel at the fair.

I hope he comes down here soon
so he can tell us about the moon!

Demelza Prisk (12)

MOON TRAIN

There is a moon train
that travels the moon.

Collecting people from
mid-night till noon.

If you could hear it
it would go *choo, choo*

If you could see it
it would look mighty fine.

So I could travel the moon
from midnight till noon . . .

Richard Wright (12)

THE SEA

We went down to the seaside for a day.
I went with my mum and dad.
We watched the waves crash up the beach like big
white teeth.
The sun was like a big round football.
The water was as cold as ice.
We went to get some ice cream.
But the seagulls came along and swooped our
ice-cream off our cones.
We had a sandcastle competition.
We won it because we were the only ones in it.
I went back into the water.
I thought I was a block of ice.
When I got out.
I couldn't find my towel.
I had to lie in the warm sand to get dry.
We got out the picnic.
We found a little white mouse eating our food.
I just dried off and it started to rain.
So we ran back to our metal machine.

Joe Lorys (11)

UP THERE ON THE MOON . . .

Up there on the moon,
Floating like a balloon.
There's no need to run
It's so much fun.
All you do is roll and bounce
And you don't even weigh an ounce!

James Farmer (12)

ALIENS

Aliens here, there, everywhere,
Running after everyone,
Eating little kiddies,
Everyone is dead.

They're coming in my house all the time,
They've burnt the rest down,
They're living in the graveyards,
Everyone is dead.

Now they're in my house,
They have eaten up my dad,
They're watching my TV,
Everyone is dead.
Except for me.

Morgan Wildman (11)

THE MOON'S A CHEESE!

The moon's a cheese, so soft, so fair
You can almost grate it way up there.
If you stand you're sure to make a print
Oh! I wish I could just have a glimpse.

The mice have nibbled where the grates are,
Don't! You're sure to sink if you take a car.
You feel like you're swimming in the sea
No gravity to pull you down
No door to turn a key . . . !

Jenna Matthews (12)

My Mum My Dad - My Dog And Me . . .

We went for a walk along the beach
My mum, my dad, my dog and me.
We looked to see what we could see
My mum, my dad, my dog and me.

We saw some people in the sea
My mum, my dad, my dog and me.
We saw some dogs running on the sand
My mum, my dad, my dog and me.

Another dog is joining in
That dog is ours - as we can see!

My mum, my dad, my dog and me!

Philip Thomson (11)

Moon Sailor

There was a moon sailor
That sailed across the moon.
Over the dusty surface
From midnight till noon.

One day he sailed into a crater
And stayed there until
Some time later . . .

He cried for help
But nobody was to be seen.
So he put on his swim suit
And dived into the sea!

Jamie Gill (12)

SPARKY

My pony is the fattest beast
that you've ever seen from west to east.

I would say he goes as fast as grease lightning
But you wouldn't believe that until
you've seen him and got it in writing.

When he stands on top of my foot
I get as mad as a March hare.
And when I forget to give him a cuddle
he stops and gives me a glare.

When I stroke my pony he is as soft as a baby's bottom
and when I forget to give him a polo
he thinks I'm extremely rotten!

Rosanna Berryman (11)

GOODBYE!

I'm lying in my bed,
with darkness around my head,
Why oh why, do we have to say goodbye.
To the shining spring and smashing summer.
Playing on the beach splashing each other.
Why oh why, do we have to say goodbye.
To the lovely summer barbie and the rich
beach parties.
Why oh why, do we have to say goodbye.
To the nice ice lollies shining in my eye
and the rich fruity sensation that makes me
feel like heaven.
Why oh why, do we have to say hi!
to the wet, cold and windy *winter!*

Catherine Hicks (11)

FOOTSTEPS...

Dark, silence
alone.
Door opens
huge footsteps
shouting
a bang
door shuts.
Running, screaming
teacher's coming
blocked in
run, run, where!
Dark
can't see
no windows
footsteps
closer, in front.
Shouting
hair pulling
footsteps go
still alone
dark, silence.
Door slams
Do what!
Go where?
Stuck
forever
footsteps
Never...!

Sara Jane Smith (11)

THE ROCKING CHAIR

She sits rocking backwards and forwards.
The roaring fire in her enlightened eyes.
Her work-worn hands click the needle knitting in and out.
The rich colours of her past surround her.

Through the window at her side
The wind whirls.
Crisp cold air creeps into every crack.
The black silhouetted trees shake and whisper
deprived of their beauty.
The grey sun shrivels and dies.
Contained by the dark icy skies.

The land is smothered with snow,
It lies still and silent with a deceiving friendly glow.
It's fresh, sharp fingers grab every ray of warmth,
Cold thoughts are melted by the awaiting flickering fire.

With her rosy, glowing cheeks and her heart warmed.
She gets up leaving her chair rocking backwards and forwards.
She pauses before the window.
She looks out and hears the front gate knocking.
She squints at the white coloured horizon
And thinks of a different season . . . spring!

As she sits back in her chair
Spring begins in her minds eye.
She thinks of a new beginning painted with yellow and blue.
A new season, when her first grand-daughter will be born.
Dreaming she falls asleep
still rocking gently between
winter and spring . . . !

Hannah Jefferies (13)

MILO THE CAT

Milo the cat went to live on the moon,
He hopped in the rocket when the engines went boom,
And he made his home by an old spoon,
Under the safety of a barrage balloon.

Soon poor Milo was spotted and found,
He was told off and his beating was sound,
They wanted to take him back to the ground,
But the first cat on the Moon little Milo was crowned.

Every time astronauts got there they'd play
Laugh loudly, sing songs and dance till midday,
Back home by his spoon little Milo would stay,
So he went to live on the Earth for a day.

So he went back to Earth,
Lived a happy life there,
Had a wife, five kids,
Quite a generous share.
But every day back
To the Moon he would stare,
So he decided to take
His family up there.

Adam Power (12)

A POEM ABOUT POEMS

A poem could be long, short or fat.
It could be funny, serious or a bit of both.
It could be happy, sad or silly.
It could rhyme or be an acrostic.
It could be about anything, and does not have to make sense.
It could be about school, or another country.
Just write freely!

Craig Matthews

DOLPHINS

Beautiful creature dives
Beautiful creature survives.

In and out of salty caves
In and out of salty waves.

Playful as can be
Playful as the sea.

Hide and seek a favourite game
Hide and seek it's always played the same.

Jumping up and down
Jumping without a frown.

In zoos they look sad
In zoos they look mad.

In the wild they look so happy
In the wild they look a bit flappy.

Don't beat them
Don't eat them!

To them you should admire
To them even if they expire!

Emma Richards (11)

THE SWEETS

Whenever children go to the sweet shop
They come out of the door
With bags and bags of sherbet.
Then when they get home
They have to take half back
And get their money back.

Adam Roberts (11)

CAMP

We're in the big dark woods
and here we're going to camp
for two whole days I have to last.

I'll never make it!

We're pitching our tents
so we can go inside
and have a good nights rest
before the next day.

I'm in my canoe now
and it's just started to rain!
I've just crashed into a bush
I think I'll get out again.

It's night-time now
and we're telling ghost stories.
We're eating marshmallows
then we'll go to bed.

Today we're going home
to see our mums and dads,
and it'll probably rain.

Was I right or was I right?
It rained all the way home . . .

Jennifer Lawry (12)

WHAT IF . . . ?

Last night while I lay thinking here,
Some 'what if's' crawled inside my ear.
And pranced and partied all night long,
And sang their same old 'what if' song.
What if I forget my books?
What if I don't have the looks?
What if my mum turns into a mouse?
What if a dinosaur squashes my house?
What if Jumbo gives me beats?
What if I have smelly feet?
What if my pen runs out of ink?
What if my brother falls down the sink?
What if I fall off my chair?
What if I lose all my hair?
What if I don't make a friend?
What if I go round the bend?
What if I can't hack the pace?
What if I fall flat on my face?
What if I can't remember that song?
What if I get the spelling test wrong?
This is obviously the worst night,
The 'what if's' really gave me a fright.
Everything seems swell and then . . .
The night-time 'what if's' strike again!

Amy Ruffell (12)

MY PARENTS ARE ALIENS

My mum and dad are aliens
They come from outer space
They've come down to examine
The cult of the human race.

My brother is an alien
He sleeps in the kitchen sink
I came down in the morning
He was an ugly shade of pink.

My sister is an alien
She's made of cotton wool
When I want to see her
She's at the bottom of our pool.

My family are all aliens
They come from outer space
They've come down to examine
The cult of the human race.

Danielle Curnow (11)

DRINK

It was cold in there and dark.
Then the light came on and I was picked up.
My cool body runs, and pours into something.
Cold stones are dropped on me.
A pipe is stabbed into me and my blood sucked.
I have been half killed, dying in the sun.

James Pool (15)

SILVER STAR

Shining silver through the night,
Pushing darkness out of sight,
Uncovering new worlds never seen,
Shining where night has always been.

Burning hot to touch and feel,
Heating you from head to heel,
Touching everything as it spreads,
Even warming the old and dead.

One of millions in the sky,
As one is born another dies,
Its light travels from near to far,
Always shining from the silver star.

Harry Penhaul (12)

ADDICTION

Attraction, giggles, smiles,
crush, a gift from God.
Desire, fantasy, lust.
His scent, warm, musky, masculine.
His hands, soft, gentle, but firm.
Longing for his touch.
Tingly, passion, steamy.
The excitement, thrills.
Body heat, noise, heavy breathing.
Ecstasy, coming down.
Satisfaction, comfort, safe.
Secure, sleep, cosy, loved.
Questions.
Right, start again!

Roxanne Thomas (15)

MIGRATION

The chilling weather approaches
Suddenly our numbers increase
We soar up in the sky
Sweeping over the Earth
Like a cloud of dots
The world beneath us
far away.
For days we survive
the weird and unknown.
Giant-like creatures,
the gale force winds.

Bright, warmth, safe
Our journey's ended.

Lindsey Richards (15)

REVENGE

One match
drifts closer to its
keeper. It's her revenge.
One strike and a spark is
born. One spark and a flame
grows. One flame and a fire burns.
Damage, destruction, fear, pain, silence,
she has now succeeded. One fire swallows
her memories, her comfort, her home, her sister.

Caroline Hunter (15)

SOMEWHERE

I looked here
I looked there
Everyone's got one
Even the weird people
I've got to have one
It's everything to me
Commando, pilot, architect, dustman
No matter what you are
You've got one
So where's mine
What is it? Be good!
It's my future . . .

Richard Sharp (15)

CLOCK

You always look at me,
Sometimes with happiness,
Sometimes with pain.
I get dizzy just lying here
As my mind spins round and round.
I'm slowly dying.
My hands need a rest.
I wait for the moment
When the batteries die.
Tick, tock. Tick, tock.
Tick, tock. Tick, tock.

Becci Bryant (15)

EARTHQUAKE

Everything going ahead as normal.
The world is alive and buzzing with
activity.
A siren starts to wail.
A wobble, a shake.
Everything stops.
Chaos breaks out.
Cracks in the roads, cracks in the walls.
People buried alive,
people dead and crushed,
people screaming with fear,
others screaming with woe.

Jonathan Bird (15)

FINAL CHAPTER

We slave,
try to make ends meet,
try to find some money.
We're left on our own, visited once in a while,
look back at all the memories, the long lost loves,
remorse and regret.
You're better up there, you're never coming back any more
I'll be there soon.

Treve James (15)

HOLLYWOOD

She left full of life,
happy, for the flicks.
Two hours of horror
and joy. Settling down
with excitement and
anticipation. The lights lower,
tension fills the air, film
rolls, with blood, death.
Screams and flesh ripping,
gore. Lights raise, she
drags herself away,
frail, drained of life.

Nicholas Welch (15)

THE TRAMP

Morning again
I wake up cold and damp
from the early morning dew.
With my dog by my side and the remains of
my past life under my arm, I gather up my
bedding before I am moved on by society.
Eventually I settle somewhere else.
It is night again.

Matthew Williams (15)

POOH BEAR

Golden fur, red fluffy jumper.
A friend who's shy and a friend
who's a high jumper. Honey is
your favourite food, yellow and
sticky, it sticks to you. Christopher is
your best friend among the many
in 100 acre wood. Round and
tubby, can I be your best friend too?

Ronwyn Watkins (16)

BUTTERFLY

Water glides over your face,
You push off the wall.
As you spear the rippling water,
You can feel the force of the water strengthening.

With skill and grace,
You swiftly set your pace.
No splashing of the water, parting at the sides,
Lap up the feeling with a trickle down your face.

A dip and a dive,
The waves of the tide.
Like a dolphin in the sea,
To fly in the water is a sensational feeling.

In 1952 Fly was official,
The dolphin's stroke accepted
Making swimming's fantasy complete,
A dip and a dive, the waves of the tide,
Breast, Crawl, Back and now Fly.

Helen Jones (11)

WRITING A POEM

I have to write a poem,
But I don't know what to write.

Every time I pick my pen up,
The paper just says white.

I ask my mum if she could think,
Of something I could turn to ink.

'I can't help,' was her stern reply,
'Just go away, I am making a fruit pie.'

My mind was going round and round,
Crash, bang, when I found . . .

A trail of ink across my page,
Tiny footprints that made me blink.

Then out of my sight under the table,
Out into the night.

I wonder who it could have been,
Who helped me set the scene

And to write a poem which could,
Have taken till midnight.

Aimi Jeanes (12)

THE HURRICANE'S PREY

The sky outside is shades of grey,
No blue can I see.

I'm the hurricane's prey,
We're the hurricane's prey.

The houses around me,
I no longer see.

I'm the hurricane's prey,
We're the hurricane's prey.

Our brothers and sisters,
Are scared today.

I'm the hurricane's prey,
We're the hurricane's prey.

Fish I can see,
Are flying through the air.

I'm the hurricane's prey,
We're the hurricane's prey.

Flying debris,
Dead animals.

I'm the hurricane's prey,
We're the hurricane's prey.

Everything's still and quiet,
Nothing is left.

I was the hurricane's prey,
We were the hurricane's prey.

Lyndsey Webster (12)

All About My Grampy

My grampy died
He was seventy-two
He died on the 28th December
On my 11th birthday.

My grampy
Was loving and caring
He will always be in my heart and my mind
I still haven't got over his death.

The last time I saw him was on
Boxing Day
Two days before he died.

He would always get on
My gran's nerves
But I know deep, deep down
He really did love her.

Sometimes I wish that it
Hadn't have happened
But I know someday
That I will die too.

Bethany Kent (11)

SPIDER!

It's short black and hairy.
Microscopic to see.
It gives me the goosebumps,
And makes me shivery!

Its eight long legs that scutter along the ground.
Its beady black eyes looking all around.

It's silent and creepy and gives me a fright!
I hope it doesn't bump into me in the middle of the night.
With its eight long legs and beady black eyes!
It might just jump out and say . . .
Surprise!

Holly Blackbourn (11)

PEACEFULNESS

The lake ripples peacefully like a sheet of material
in the wind.
The wispy clouds float gently across the sky like
a boat on a calm sea.
The golden leaves are shrivelled and dry like
aged paper.
The mountain top is white like a pudding topped
with cream.
The trees sway in the breeze like grass
in a field.
And a lone bird calls to his partner like a
whistle through the mist.
Everywhere and everything is peaceful and it seems
that nothing can break this.

Catherine Armstrong (13)

IN THE SKY

Soft, flowing clouds,
Gliding gently through the sky
like a duck in water.

In the evening when the sun's on fire,
The beaming sunrays shimmer through the clouds
like water pouring from a watering can.

At night I lay awake under the stars,
The glistening, twinkling gems,
Against the black ash background,
Shine gently
like ripples on the moonlit water.

When I awake,
The moon submerges into emptiness,
With the sun ascending up into the clouds,
The fiery completion of the sun,
Passing the silver slick-tongued moon.

Becki Page (13)

FEARSOME SHARKS

My fear of sharks is eating me,
This certain fear won't let me be.
They're everywhere, they're in my bed,
They're in my bath and in my head.
Twenty-four hours every day,
This fear won't ever go away.
I dream about them every night,
They won't let me out of their sight.
Will I die from the fear?
Or will my head soon be clear?

Kerri Thomas (13)

VOLCANO

Rivers of fire, pouring, smothering,
Barren bare land, destruction, kills all life.
Rolling balls of dust, fuming, consuming,
Ashes falling, like a moonscape, darkness.

Lava lakes with awesome power, ooze,
The blood of the earth, pours steaming.
Lava rocks fall from the sky, flattening,
Overwhelming, waterfalls of lava.

Sulphur smells and poisonous gases,
Painful, gritty dust that makes you ill.
Smoky, explosive like fireworks, *boom!*
The showers of autumn colours shine.

The lava flows to the coast,
Digging a deep canyon as it goes,
Spilling over rocks into its water grave,
Sizzling as it meets the deep blue sea.

Melissa Gibson (13)

GENTLE

Gentle is a river,
Flowing on its way,
Down, down and beyond,
Towards the sparkling sea.

Gentle is a kite,
Flying high in the sky,
Floating in the breeze,
Attached only by a single thread.

Gentle is a boat,
Bobbing on the ocean,
Tossing around and about,
Hurrying on its way.

Gentle is a baby's touch,
Its pink soft skin,
Delicately searching for objects,
Soothing everything it finds.

Elizabeth Armstrong (13)

My Monster!

Mum!
There's a monster under my bed,
it's yellow and hairy and it's got a purple head!
It's got big googly eyes and a funny shaped nose,
and when I'm asleep I'm afraid where it goes!

It might be in my cupboard or even behind the door,
and I can't go to sleep because I don't like dreaming anymore!
If it's behind the door then squash it like a fly, but if it's in
the cupboard then we'll just have to hide!

Mum!
I saw my monster last night,
and guess what, he didn't give me a fright!
He spoke to me and asked what the fuss is all about,
I said I thought he'd eat me and then spit me out!

He laughed and said 'No not I!'
and then I just had to ask him why?
He said 'I'm a vegetarian, I'd never eat you, but I'll have some
Soya dumplings with some fried tofu!'

Alex Parks (14)

SUBWAY

This subway in the city,
It's very busy there,
A poor old man is shivering away,
He's not welcome anywhere.

His bed is made of litter,
His clothes are only rags,
His only most valued possession,
Is a packet of Silk Cut fags.

He keeps his beer close by his side,
Like a comfort for his fear,
He stays here all day, all night,
Yet never sheds a tear.

He has no money in the world,
His life is pretty dead,
His tangled hair like a bird's nest,
Sits crazily on his head.

He lives his life in the subway,
People pass him every day,
No one has the time to share,
As his mind slowly drifts away . . .

Jessica Impey (12)

AUTUMN DAYS

Blazing colours cover the trees,
Of orange, red and yellow leaves.
As the wind rustles and blows,
Piles of leaves begin to grow.

I hear crispy, crackly sounds,
As I walk along the colourful ground.
Leaves get kicked high in the sky,
While I watch people walk on by.

Gemma Collett (13)

GENTLE

Gentleness is like a shy withdrawn whisper,
reminding me of a delicate beauty,
her hair so fair and tumbling,
She is a graceful dancer,
entwining her gossamer wings around all roughness.

Enchanted we watch her elegantly moving,
her arms milk-white and dainty,
She touches our hearts and rests our emotions,
Making every breath more delicate,
Our very souls uplifted by her purity.

The movements she makes are hardly heard,
as she tiptoes around in the night,
her wand twinkling with her eyes,
She gazes onto all life and quells it,
to stillness like an empty subconscious.

Gently she melts into the darkness,
her smooth and pure figure,
we witness her whiteness drifting away,
feeling a peace of mind left behind,
her power cannot be described,
as less than . . . magical.

Kathryn Easlick (14)

AUTUMN CANVAS

Larch woods make shades of a golden flame,
Michaelmas daisies stand splendid in full flower,
Showing pure pointilism, in pink and mauve.
Old man's beard nods sagely in the rushing wind.
Woody nightshade bears blooms of cardinal red and ochre.
Hips and haws make splashes of crimson,
Bright in the viridian hedgerows.
The burnt sienna branches of tall oak trees
Are ready to yield their two-tonal fruit.
Hazel nuts are dappled a deep sepia
And the beech mast of the beech tree is ripe and plump.
The berries of a guelder-rose boast vermilion,
Yet on the rowans they are timid orange.
On the brambles the berries are ebony black.
Slowly but surely the landscape transmutes,
Turning the land into a myriad of colour,
Which takes shape on the canvas of the inner eye.

Rebecca Hitchens (14)

KILL FOR FUN

The fox can run but it can't hide,
The hounds are snapping at his feet,
As he runs on at an amazing pace,
He knows he's going to be meat.
He can hear the hounds are panting,
There's a river up ahead,
The hounds are slowly catching up,
He knows they want him dead.
The hunters are all cheering,
They're going to have his head,
A flash of claws and sharp white teeth,
The river's running red.

Leo Anderson (12)

CURRENT FEARS, OR FUTURE MEMORIES?

Don't eat crisps in the corridor.
Stand back and mind the queues.
Tuck your shirt in straight away.
Do you have a pass for those shoes?
Sorry I'm late everybody,
Is that three rings I can see?
If I can do it, you can.
Who threw that rubber at me?
Have you *no* manners, Katy!
Don't be afraid to ask
You crowd, stop clowning around,
Get on and finish the task.
Who hasn't done the homework?
Own up and let me see.
Stand, choir, and now be seated.
I've got green cards with me.

Emmie Partington (13)

FEARSOME

When I was small
the one thing I was
mostly afraid of was
The dark!
I always used to dread
the time when my mum
would come and say
goodnight.
Because that meant
the light had to go off!
I just lay there until eventually
I started to very slowly
fall asleep . . .

Emma Almey (11)

SPIDER

I am standing here
with a magnifying glass
looking at the spider.

He has six glazed eyes
and eight hairy legs
looking at the spider.

He looks really big
but he is really small
looking at the spider.

Some have venom
some are harmless
looking at the spider.

James Rowberry (13)

FALLING LEAVES AND DUSTY WINDS

Falling leaves and dusty winds,
Whistling through the hollow trees,
The sound of death,
It lurks around,
It hides behind the musky sound.

The falling leaves of autumn,
Brown, orange and red,
Slowly dropping to the ground,
All withered, dry and dead.

Tom Dominé (13)

THE VOLCANO

The powerful thundering sounds,
Terrified villagers,
Forced to flee,
All they own, wiped out,
As their houses join the ongoing mass of lava.

The flowing oozing rivers,
Waterfalls of lava,
A mass of magma,
Spat from the belly of the volcano,
Like a rain of terror.

Walking through the ash,
Clouds of grey,
Inches deep,
Like a moonscape,
Like traipsing through snow.

The crumbling cliff
Remains of the dead,
Bones, skulls,
A rain of ash, made worse by winds,
A terrorizing sandstorm.

The natural killer volcano.

Amy Bucknole (12)

BLOOD OF THE EARTH

Skin peeling intense heat
Splash of eye-burning red
Fills the sky and cascades
Into the silence and mist
Of the unknown.
The lava is like an ocean
Spray of blood-red and
Fiery orange and chaos-black.
A mountain of steaming ash
A deadly cocktail of ash
And lava.
Ash falls like a blizzard in
The far distance of an autumn night.
The sound is like a cacophony of
Roaring, howling and hissing.
The taste of burnt sulphur lingers like
Snow in the depth of your mouth.
The steam scalds your fingers and
Your palms are scarred with blisters
And boils.
The smell is like a furnace of plastic
Burning your nose hairs off and
Clinging to them like superglue.
The ash falls like snow over
The grassy verges and trees.
The lava is the blood of
The Earth.

Lewis Baker (15)

WAKING UP TO REALITY

I had a dream,
A cold heartless dream,
Of a world in desperate despair.
Guns blazing, shells dropping, bombs pounding,
Like a fuming fiery hell.
Stupid, senseless, slaughter of men killing men.
The effects of war.

Soldiers, lying with lost limbs,
Deep red blood oozing, trickling, spurting.
Intense, unbearable agony of innocent victims,
Some lying motionless, all life disappeared.
The agony for them has passed,
The pain for their loved ones has just begun,
Wives without husbands,
Children without fathers,
Mothers without sons.
The effects of war.

Houses humbled to rock, rubble, and ruin.
Nowhere to stay,
Nowhere to sleep,
No way to survive.
Families fearing for the future,
Foraging for food, like unwanted strays.
Struggling to eat,
Struggling to keep warm,
Struggling to exist.
The effects of war.

I woke up from my dream,
My cold heartless dream,
To find the world in desperate despair.

David Wills (14)

MY FEARSOME TEACHER

I used to have a fearsome teacher,
He would shout at us all day long.
He would get angry, go red and start to sweat,
Then his armpits would begin to pong.

I used to have a fearsome teacher,
Of whom everybody would be scared.
Louder and louder his shouting would get,
I really wonder if he actually cared.

I used to have a fearsome teacher,
Much homework he did give to us.
It was too much to do in one day,
And it had to be finished off on the bus.

I used to have a fearsome teacher,
On a field trip we did go,
To see a volcano burst and erupt,
Boy, did that thing blow.

I used to have a fearsome teacher,
On the volcano side he did trip.
We ran away from the oncoming lava,
And into it his body began to slip.

I used to have a fearsome teacher,
But now he's gone and dead.
Now we have a female teacher,
She's not fearsome but kind instead.

Alex Whitman (15)

I'VE HEARD STORIES

As I awake
With midnight near
I pull back the curtains
The dark brings me fear

The moon is out
The stars they shine
But in the distance
I can hear a sigh

Is it the wind
That makes the floor creak
Or is it a voice
That quietly speaks

I've heard stories
Of ghosts and ghouls
That when midnight strikes
It's the witches who rule

Goblins and fiends
Planning attacks
On innocent children
Behind their backs

Magic and spells
Warlocks will cast
Transforming butterflies
To furry black rats

As the dark devours
The living dead
It all gets too much
And I get back into bed.

Jessica Wallwork (14)

VOLCANO

A stream of lava hurtling towards you,
A mountain of deadly falling rocks,
A red-hot devil with an upset stomach,
You're going to be swallowed by lava.

Choking on the dust and ash,
Breathing the whispy smoke,
Inhaling the poisonous gases,
Tasting the blackened soot.

Its amazing beauty is deadly,
Its mudslides scream disaster,
Its lava pools mumble 'Get moving,'
The shaking mountain shouts 'Run!'

An overflowing lake of fire,
Bombarding towards you at speed,
A fountain of rocks and lava,
Sprinkle you with an orange glow.

The burning taste of dust,
The smoky ash of death,
The angry roar of hell,
You've reached the devil's playground.

Hanna Lewis (12)

A FEARSOME BEAUTIFUL FRENZY

It begins
a careless thought
a lack of respect for life.
The red flower blooms
into an onslaught of destruction
It spreads through the buildings
caressing the foundations in flame
relieving the tired timber
of supporting the massive structure.
It rushes through the building
cleansing all life of worry and monotony,
glass shatters into an array of poisoned sparkles.
The tired building rests and dies a beautiful death
a spectrum of colour unfolds from within
and then silence.
The writhing orange beast can no longer rise
The great beauty reduced to only delicate flame
The sparks, once so beautiful in the maelstrom
are now gnarled fragments laid to rest.
Mighty automobiles now overturned into twisted metal,
bodies litter the ground
children, the elderly
those who we would strive to protect.
A grand victory for the cult heroes who fight for their people
But the people . . . are dead.
When all is said and done, we find that this slaughter
is nothing but a fearsome beautiful frenzy.

Ian Bucknole (14)

NIGHTMARE

She gallops softly through your mind,
Her white tail blowing in your thoughts,
Then her echoing cry feeds your imagination,

She hears a dripping noise it alerts her,
So ears pricked, tail high,
She wanders through your mind,
The noise is a dream dripping from your imagination,
Into a colourful puddle,
The dream is being watched,
By the nightmare.

Her flowing tail turns into a mass of nettles,
Her white coat turns black,
She entwines the dream in her tail,
The dream's soft shell breaks,
The dream turns into a nightmare,
The nightmare gallops from your mind,

She leaves your thoughts and imagination,
To take the nightmare,
Take it where?
No one knows.

Alexandra Ryan (13)

BULLFIGHTING

The audience laugh and glare and stare
The bull completely unaware
I wish one day the bull will turn
And for the matador's blood will yearn.

I wish one day they would realise
How I and friends do despise
Why do they do it for people's fun?
What have the bulls ever done?

They tease to please
The moment to seize
The matador lunges to stab in the back
The guilty kill of an attack.

The war has ended
All is done
But the guilt lies
Within us.

Anouska House (12)

FEARSOME

I see, I hear, I know
they're here,
In my house somewhere
near,
I hear them breathing,
I see them touching,
I am hiding, I am crouching.

I see, I hear, I know they're here,
They are getting near, I can see from
here,
I hear them bellow, I hear them
clamour, I cry out but now they're
here.

I see, I hear, I know they're here,
They've found me and I
fear,
They tear me limb from
limb,
I wake up with dribble on
my chin.

Andrew Whitefield (13)

FEAR

As I walked along the landing
To the dreaded bed,
My mum walked up behind me,
Come on it's in your head.

I cuddled in the bedclothes,
As mum turned out the light,
Afraid the ghosts and ghoolies,
Would come again tonight.

I looked into the corner,
A ghost was standing there,
As I looked at it I saw
Its long glowing silver hair.

Creep into the darkness,
I walk in through the dark,
See the ghostly doggy,
Hear his ghostly bark.

Crept to the doorway,
Turned on the light,
Looked into the mirror,
I was white with fright.

Jade Orrowe (12)

THE DARK

I am darkness I am achromatic,
I can be colossal yet diminutive,
You can't hear me, see me nor touch me.

I exist for many reasons,
I live for command of the souls,
I command the unrestrained shadows of the night.

I am intimidating and deadly,
I rule each world for twelve hours a day
I am the enemy of the people who fear the night.

Many people fear me but it's understandable,
As they walk down the dusky streets at night,
I watch causing them to boil with fear.

I am menacing, cold and frightening,
I live for anarchy and the judgement of the souls,
I am darkness I am fearsome.

I make people have deathly visions,
People can see their own fate,
Or even experience their own fate.

I am darkness I am achromatic,
I can be colossal yet diminutive,
You can't hear me, see me, nor touch me.

Kieran Wilson (14)

FEARSOME FROLICS

One night
When the light was out
And I was in my bed,
I woke up with a fright
To find a monster bash.
The shockers were
A-rocking
And the DJ
Was the devil,
And the elves were a-rapping
And the ghosts were a-clapping.
The witches were doing the conga
And the zombies could dance no longer.
The goblins were break-dancing.
The demons were morris dancing.
I started tap dancing
And they all started laughing.

Michael Buck (11)

AUTUMN

Sunsets over barren lands
Wind stirring leaves already dead
Colours sensual, passionate, stunning,
But tears fill my eyes instead.

The summer's over now.
The leaves turn golden on the trees.
Dead, bare branches gently sway
In the bitter winter breeze.

I know ahead the ground is bare
As once it used to be.
The sun is now behind me
And my shadow's all I see.

Winter freezes nostalgic tears
That an autumn may bring.
I'll dry the tears that once I cried,
I can feel the warmth of spring.

Julie Bennett (15)

MAGICAL SPELL OF AUTUMN

Leaves,
Burnt brown by the summer's sun,
Crowned with gold,
Rustling as the wind gushes about,
The magical air of autumn.

A carpet of leaves
That have fallen
From the bare trees
That stand tall.

A damp landscape
Losing its life,
Yet the spell of its season
Is still keeping winter in suspense

Until each leaf has fallen,
Each tree is bare,
The damp has settled.
Only then will the magical spell of autumn
With one sad rainbow
Disappear.

Janine Gladwell (13)

LOOKING BACK

Looking back at the pain in my heart,
The crying in my eyes which was everlasting,
The agonising stabbing in my stomach,
Worrying about how and where.
The lying and the hurt,
My eyes filling with tears.

Looking back, knowing I was going to leave my home,
The place where I was born,
The place where I had all my memories and happiness,
Where neighbours held us tight and told us stories,
Which was where there was unquestionable light.

Who knows what we are doing now?
Moving from house to house, no money, no friends,
With a world full of strangers.

The friends that were so kind and precious have now gone.
The life I had has now disappeared and vanished.
As I sleep in the gloom, all I have left are those memories I had so long
ago.

Helen Wyatt (13)

THE FOOD ARTIST
(After Seamus Heaney)

My father worked with many foods,
Creating masterpieces to feed
The many hundreds of people
Spending money on their greed.

An expert. He would cook to perfection
In order to please, placing everything
Neatly, as if a machine.
Bright colours, pretty shapes, just like a painting.

I wanted to grow up and cook.
Become well known for my talent.
All I ever did was look
And occasionally used the kitchen balance.

I was a nuisance, following, questioning
His speedy actions with food.
But today it is my father who's asking
About my life, 'for my own good'.

Samantha Beard (15)

MEMORIES: FLIGHT NIGHT

At the airport, feeling tremendously ill,
The foreign doctor had prescribed one pill.
I felt so awful; I wanted to die,
He'd told me I'd be okay to fly.

Carrying my bag, feeling tired and unfit,
Departure lounge crowded, there's nowhere to sit.
My head is in pieces, my world's spinning round,
I slump to the floor; collapsed on the ground.

In the plane now, feeling all on my own,
Falling asleep to the aeroplane's drone.
Wake up over London, late in the night,
And now it begins, my biggest fright.

The pressure drops quickly, heightening my fear,
The infection starts raging, within my right ear.
An axe through the air, cutting deep in my head,
The pain so intense, I'd rather be dead.

I have to keep going, there's no turning back,
But the noise gets louder . . .
. . . And then it goes black.

Roger Picton (15)

SHADES OF AUTUMN

The skeletal leaves whirl down towards the accumulating mound
beneath,
They almost shriek as the gentle breeze carries them far away; to their
destined peril.
Leaving entwined branches naked, shivering in the bleak, dusky air.
Where absent minded being trample and strike the bony structures,
Not as much caring as distressing as the thick mud oozes between their
grimy toes.

The sweltering ball of fire descends, casting gloomy shades, as if to
join the solitary leaves.
The tranquil silence is suddenly disrupted with the intense crows of a
neighbouring cockerel, piercing the silent air.
The dew clings to the lean single blades blowing in the now gusting
wind.
The lingering stench plagues the air from the chicken coop.
The pattering of rain is heard in the distance.
The rain falls and licks every leaf with a separate tone of every shade.

Megan Shaw

DAD

Out in the morning bright as a lark.
Check over the tractor before you start.
Ploughing today says the boss from the door.
Up and down the fields all day.
Glad when it's too dark to see any more.
Back in the yard put all away.
Jump in the van and away home.
Another day done.

Tamzine Ford (12)

STORM

Smashing, crashing,
lapping over the harbour
wall, like the side of your
bath when you get in.

Slashing around a
seafront shop, like a
hosepipe spraying on
a patio.

Water seeping under
a shop door, like
a thief sneaking in.

Cars driving through a
torrent of water like
a snowplough pushing
its way through.

People dashing through
the pouring rain to shelter
like ants rushing to a
fresh piece of apple, trying
to get home,
out of the storm.

Sophie Gekas (12)

VOLCANO

The sea of fire
Destructive, commanding
Nothing can stop it
The Earth's big oven.

Grey clouds of dust
Shooting through the air
Covering the landscape
Like snow, in winter.

The black falling rocks
And lava flowing down
The orange sludge, beautiful
Like waterfalls of fire.

The dust, like mists
Of poisonous sulphur
Is what you breathe in
On this mountain of death.

The loud sizzling noise
Like hot pans in water
The sounds of fireworks exploding
But louder and much much bigger.

The sea of fire stops
But Earth looks like another planet
Like the moon's surface
But covered in ash.

Oscar Smith (12)

THE BULLY!

Living in a world of depression and fear,
The curtains are drawn behind closed eyes,
And no one can hear my screams or cries.
Reaching out to passers-by who, with every good intention,
Just choose to turn away,
Not even to mention . . .
The physical and mental scars, I bury deep inside.
Is it any wonder I cower down and hide?
It doesn't matter who I am, what's happening to me and why?
My sorrows are drowned beneath me,
Which leave puddles as I cry.
Impassioned thoughts flow through my mind, they will not go away,
As distorted shadows tower above which block the light of day.
I see the eyes of danger,
What I've done I do not know.
My frozen body indicates,
The season's winter's snow.
My head is pounding, and always this damn persistent hum!
From fierce and savage beatings, my mind is blank,
And body numb.
Will there ever be a time when I can be happy and contented?
The feelings that I feel right now are;
Ridicule, teased, tormented.
Wouldn't anyone like me who felt lonely, abused and used,
Who are frightened now of living,
But then . . .
That's for me to choose!

Sharon Moyle (15)

VOLCANOES

Lava exploding into the air,
Like ferocious fireworks, red hot
With anger.
The lava bubbles like a
Witch's concoction in a cauldron.

Lava flowing like a river,
Destroying anything in its path,
Slowly the lava forms into
Lakes spitting out heat like
A fire-breathing dragon.

Waves of lava crash up
Against flaking rocks,
Then slowly the sea cools,
The lava cools down and turns
It into stone-cold black basalt.

Suddenly the volcano belches out
A big cloud of smoke.
Filling the skies, the smoke
Forms into statues, then slowly
It falls from the skies.

As it reaches the ground,
It creates a duvet of
Dust, feet thick and torturous
To walk in, like red
Hot burning coal.

Anthony Booth (13)

The Wrong Side Of The Tracks

Leaving the light, the last safe place,
entering the darkness,
who knows what lies there.

Smooth pavement underfoot turns to broken rubble,
Nice terraces with neat gardens turn to grotty semi-detached
houses with boarded-up windows,
Cars on brick podiums stand like guards,
and a hundred pairs of eyes peer between the window slats.

This neighbourhood looks deserted, but it isn't,
you know it isn't,
there are lots of muggings around here, violent,
even some killings.

You start to panic,
Your mind races, you start to run,
You can see the light of better neighbourhoods
up ahead,
and start to sprint.

You reach the light and stop to catch your breath,
Start to calm down,
look back into the darkness but there's nothing to
worry about,
you're safe now.

Matthew Ferran (13)

AUTUMN

In cloudless sunshine overhead
A change whispers in the breeze,
The sound of whistling birds in the sky.
Autumn lives, summer dies
As evening comes
The sunset sky,
A spectrum of colours in the clouds pass by.
Sombre leaves turn green to red
The ground is now their resting bed.
Ivy crawls up the trees.
Moss nestles in every crevice.
Cool shadows rest on leafy ground
As orchard boughs form their dying mounds.
Sunflowers mark the golden hours,
Moors covered by precious purple flowers.
As we gather in the silver streams
We go to sleep with moonlit dreams.

Emma-Jane Howman (16)

CADAVER OF AUTUMN

At last summer's tired
The clouds are flocking in
As I walk down the leaf-plagued streets
The leaves swirling like a shoal of fraught fish
The frost crunches under my feet
As I walk across the crisp-biscuit grass.
Can I find my way
Through this never-ending smoky mantle?
The dewy grass crumples and cracks as I bear down on it.
The cadaver of autumn lays still, as still as death.

Tim Tregear (14)

SOMME AUTUMN

Struggling through the rancid mud,
A vain attempt to gain control.
Their strange cries fill me with dread
As they move in stubborn advance.
A screeching bird flies towards me
And I throw my face in the mud.

As it flies clear of me it makes
One last giant call. I hear my
Comrades scream out in agony.
Then the heavy shower of hail
Crashes to the ground around me.
I dive head first into shelter.

Above me the wind sears the flesh
Of those who were caught in the storm.
I optimistically look
Out of my hole and see the
Dark mist swirl in, propelled by wind.
I cover my face in my scarf.

As darkness envelops the land
Shooting stars thwart its death-like grip.
Badgers, clad in black, snoop around,
Poking their noses everywhere.
Even under blackness the leaves
Fall off the trees in swirls of red.

Matthew Taylor (15)

AUTUMN PERSONIFIED

With her long, golden cloak flowing behind her,
She wanders silently through the wood,
Her intention unknown.
She approaches a small, young tree,
And with her pale outstretched hand,
She gently touches a leaf.
It starts to curl and die.
As it falls it turns from a
Rich green to a dismal brown.
She smiles to herself,
Her eyes gleaming with mischief,
As she carries on searching.
She draws near to a delicate cobweb
And breathes upon it, her liquid breath
Baptising it with tiny droplets of water,
That glimmer in the faint light,
And filters through the trees.
Satisfied, she moves on.
Her eyes shine when she stumbles upon a mouse,
Hiding beneath the dead leaves.
She waves her hand, as if casting a spell.
Immediately the mouse falls into a deep sleep,
And will not awake until spring.
Having fulfilled her purpose she turns,
And walks slowly into the enshrouding mist.

Laura Dunsdon (14)

I'M NOT GOING TO WRITE
ABOUT AUTUMN

I don't think I'll mention the mist,
Mystifying valleys below.
Swallowing up cities and houses and trees,
Nor the dew-ridden cobwebs that glow.

I'm not going to write about autumn.

I'm not going to include the leaves,
Dropping from tree upon tree up high.
Rustic yellows, reds, golds and browns,
Falling to earth with a sigh.

I'm not going to write about autumn.

I don't like the idea of days,
Shorter and shorter as they grow.
Closing us in, trapped in the morning,
The nights spent by fireside glow.

I'm not going to write about autumn.

Miss Autumn sweeps over the land,
Squeezing life from the roots.
With her black veil, and cloak sweeping wide,
Destruction the phrase that she moots.

. . . I can't write about autumn!

Billy Headdon (15)

VOLCANOES

Look out, look out there's a volcano coming,
It's crashing down the rocks with lots of noise.
Ash everywhere, smoke, smog and poisonous gases,
Ash keeps falling, the smoke getting blacker and blacker,
It's getting darker and the noise is getting louder.

The heat is great, reaching at least 1100°C,
The lava is blindingly bright, yellow, orange and red.
The stream of lava travelling at a great speed
Is hot and vicious. You can hear it sizzling and
The waves from the lakes are growing bigger.

The events of the active volcano are frightening
Because the lava is glowing and exploding and
gurgles as it travels.
The columns of ash stretch for miles and the
height of it is frightening.
The gases are choking and it's so dark,
I can't see, I can hear though, I can hear the
volcano getting closer and closer.

Mark Jones (14)

MEMORIES

The sound of the bomb echoed around
As the flaming pilot fell to the ground
The German Messershmitt fled away
Relieved, today, wasn't his dying day.

The newly-wed wife of the pilot was told
As the words sank in, she turned bitterly cold
Her heart turned to stone, she cared not for life
Now only his widow - no longer his wife.

With wrinkles now spread and frown lines constant
She sits on her chair rocking memories distant
Her heart defrosts as she remembers his face
Her frown now gone and a tear in its place.

She recalls, when he laughed - how his face was a glow
And when he grinned, just slightly, how his dimples would show.
She remembers his voice and his twinkling eyes
But she can't bring him back, though she often tries.

Vicki Harris (14)

AUTUMN

As autumn closes in around me,
I feel myself being lifted into a new world;
A world of emptiness.
The wind enswirls me
As a leaf lands at my feet.
I glance up at the tree above.
Its weak, mahogany leaves being snatched by the wind,
And deposited at its foot.
As a new day breaks,
The mist settles in
And blankets its surrounding.
The soft crunch of my footsteps.
On the frost covered grass,
Are heard by the young children
Searching for conkers in the ploughed fields.
A shiver runs through me
As the cold wind strikes,
Waiting to take me to the next world.

Michael Cousins (14)

A Fright In The Night

I lay on my bed alone one night
Waiting for monsters to give me a fright.
The fear that I had was like thick, black glue,
Holding me down in a misty cocoon.

Noises came sailing through the dark;
Wailing wind and beastly barks.
Whispering witches and moaning monsters wait,
To carry me off if I don't stay awake.

But wait a moment now I can sleep,
Because the stars a twinkling watch will keep.
The moons silvery eyes will protect me now,
Because the gathering of ghosts it will not allow.

Stuart Gladwell (11)

Valley Policeman

(After Seamus Heaney)

My father worked with the bad boys,
Sending them to jail,
People screaming, loads of noise,
The handcuffs clicking on the rails.

An expert. Tall and fast,
Chasing through dark alleys,
No criminals could get past.
Watch out in the Welsh Valleys.

I wanted to run fast,
To pull the bad boy to the ground.
I only heard the clock tick past,
While my father, more criminals found.

I was a nuisance, pestering him about the job,
Always asking questions, wondering about the day.
What had happened to the drunken mob?
But today, he could not say!

Beccy Everett (15)

FEAR

When you lie there in the pitch-black
You hear a *bang, bump, crash.*
Then *creak, creak* coming up the stairs.
The sweat running down my face
The covers sticking to my legs.

The door knob turning, turning.
What could it be, who knows?
It could be the bogie man
Or a vampire to suck my blood!
Help Mum! Dad please *help!*

A light shining in who is it? What is it?
The figure entering my room.
I reach for my light I cannot find it
I found it, I press it and . . . ?

Robyn Holroyd (12)

MEMORIES

The memories are very vivid,
They're from not so long ago,
When the light had finally faded,
And left me all alone.

She always brought such happiness
To all those who were near.
Her smile and words of comfort,
They all still seem so clear.

Reminiscing all those times,
When she'd ask me about my day
Or tell me how I've grown.
It's these little things she'd say.

Should problems ever arise,
She'd always hold a remedy.
She was able to solve everything
With a whisper and a cup of tea!

And now it seems so strange,
To touch the past we thought had gone.
This flame may be extinguished,
But these memories will live on.

Sam Mawby (15)

FOLLOWER

(After Seamus Heaney)

My mother worked with a paintbrush
And steadily sketched her world.
Her hands carved tall sculptures
Of figures young and old.

An expert. She would guide her hands
And skilfully shape soft clay
In images of the surrounding lands.
She would work through night and day.

I would watch her paintbrush fly
Across each clean page.
I would share her each and every sigh
When paintings failed and her temper raged.

I wanted to grow up and paint
On canvasses large and small.
Annoying my mother was all I did,
As my paint splattered the wall.

I was a nuisance, borrowing her brushes,
Ruining them always. But today
It is my mother who leans over my shoulder
Behind me, and will not go away.

Cassandra Penn (15)

MEMORIES

I nestle back against the ancient bark of the old oak,
Nothing to do but open the album that rests upon my lap.
Memories, which were once extinguished oblivion,
Now erupt into the waves of reality.
Images of supreme achievements,
Condensed into the drops of timeless repose.
Tears of pears rounded to the extent of the earth's judgement,
Once fading away, float down the stream of life's age.
Or that's what I thought,
For now they seem to be returning,
Memories long forgotten,
Exhumed from the crust of life's surface.

Memories of the good times; fine and focused.
Memories of the bad;
Haunting the cells of the subconscious mind.
Dimensions of the longing desire
For the good memories to remain
And for the bad to depart.
For now, looking at the album of my life.
I see that once, nothing could be remembered,
But flowing through the corridor of time,
All is coming back . . .
Memories of good fortune - and not.
Golden sun, warm beaches, strawberry ice-cream;
The clichés of childish ignorance
Seem all to be true.
Returning to illness, poverty, desperation,
Assume not; for the poor can rise and become Emperors.
Memories which are willed to be forgotten
Are often dragged back through the passage of bad fortune.

Morwenna Wills (15)

MEMORIES

The mist started to climb
As the thunder crashed
And the dogs barked.
People started to move.
From the bedroom window
A light shone.

A child of six stood staring.
He saw everything.
He saw the people,
The women dressed in Victorian dresses
And the men in black suits.

The horses came after,
Click, click, click.
Suddenly all the people
Stopped and stood still,
Not moving.
Then they turned
To face the boy of six.

Soon after that there was a
Piercing scream
And the boy was never to be seen again.
Still to this day
Children dream
Of the boy who disappeared.

Jennifer Wherry (12)

MEMORIES

I had a past,
I had a face.
I had a name
To call my own
But all I have is a chair
In a retirement home,
An old rocking chair.

I have no window.
No view of life
But I can see
In my mind
Forgotten days of transfixed times.
I had a past of joyful times.

My memories snatched away.
To live my days out
As a faceless face with a chair
In a retirement home,
An old rocking chair.
But I have nothing else.
I have no feelings . . . except,
Of emptiness a silent shell.

Amy Legg (14)

THE WASHER

(After Seamus Heaney)

My mother worked with soap powder,
Her tall figure hunched up on the floor,
Down on her knees, sorting out clothes,
She sat there hidden behind the door.

An expert. She would sort the wash,
Preventing colours from mixing in.
The machine spun round, never stopped;
Everything shook because of the din.

Whenever I was poorly
I used to sneak out of my bed.
I tried to help with the sorting
But ended up turning whites red.

I wanted to be able to clean
And make all the clothes gleaming white.
I was only allowed to fold them,
But even that never went right.

I was a nuisance, shouting, playing,
Messing up clothes, ripping the knees,
But one day it may be my turn
And I'll be the one who isn't pleased.

Jenifer Henthorn (15)

THE AUTUMN SUN

In the depth of autumn,
When the air is crisp,
Is a place I go,
To think - to dream.

All the problems,
That once troubled me,
Seem to fade away
When I'm in this special place.

This beautiful sight is like no other,
The sun in all its power and glory,
Vanishing from the sight of all,
It disappears beneath the sea.

The warm evening sky,
Slowly changes from light to dark.
The mysterious deep red glow,
Overpowers the still blue sky.

Like blood dripping silently,
Into a vast deep pool,
The sun devours all light,
As day becomes night

As the sun sinks deeply
Into the red blue sea,
The enchanting red light
That once ruled the sky, goes with it.

Thomas Likeman (14)

AUTUMN

The trees sway with thin bare branches,
Which bend and curve like long, lean grass,
The sun appears in the darkened sky,
Which makes the dew on the spider web glisten.

And old tree stands, high in bracken,
Which twists and twirls around its trunk,
Suffocating the trunk from cold morning air,
Tightly wrapped around, like a present.

Its leaves have fallen,
Fallen from the branches' tight grasp,
Only to leave the tree thin and bare,
With its branches in full view.

The leaves are multicoloured and crisp,
Which are no more attached to the trees.
They just lay, still and tranquil,
Settled on the delicate, moist grass.

A cold wisp of wind whisks up the leaves,
Which makes them all crumpled and deformed,
The scaly fronds, now quiet and comfortable,
Rot away to oblivion.

Once again, the leaves are still,
Remorseful and doing no harm,
And still the tree stands high,
To face another year.

Kate Doran (14)

AUTUMN

Leaves danced,
Skilful ballerinas,
Twisting and spinning
In the crisp, cold air.
Each leaf unique
In both colour and shape,
They spin to the ground,
Aeroplanes, out of control.

One leaf twists
Out of direction
And lands in the soft, woollen gloves,
Belonging to a young child.
His two amazed, heart warming eyes,
Glare softly into the leaf
As it quietly rests,
In the little boy's hands.

The boy continues to stare
Into the bewildered leaf,
Until a sharp gust
Blows the leaf from the child
And almost at once
The leaf becomes part of the autumn descent.

Cassie Chamberlain (14)

BRUISED

He was pushing me and using me,
Like a bowling ball,
I was bruised and cut
Like the flesh of a slaughtered cow,
I had nowhere to turn,
But him.

Screaming, shouting,
Shouting out loud,
This is how I feel,
The hurting and the pain is
Like dying.

This is how I feel,
Up here in my mind,
I think about it,
All the time,
I go crazy.

I had no one to speak to,
No one to tell,
My whole world changed.

I wonder, I wonder,
If it would be better,
If he hadn't done this to me,

Ten years it's been,
Since this day,
It's much better now,
But I can't forget,
What he's done to me.

Charlene Welsh (13)

DEATH

I close my eyes and I see you.
You're in my mind all the time.
But when I allow myself to think about you,
I find myself in tears.
I can still feel the emptiness,
That you left when you died.

I can't bring myself
To cry in front of anyone.
Because I can't see how anyone,
Can understand the way I feel.
I cry myself to sleep at night,
Feeling like a part of me is dead,
Knowing I'll never see you again.

Everyone talks about you being in Heaven,
But all I know is the loneliness
I feel without you.
I miss you so much
Sometimes I just can't cope.
I want to talk to you,
And for you to give me a hug,
And tell me everything's okay.
But no matter how much I want it,
I know deep down it will never happen,
And that scares me.

Katrina Granville (14)

SWIRLING WINDS

They felt themselves being bashed,
Bashed by the force of the winds,
Winds which swirled and twisted
Around the land.

Towering above them,
The tornado ripped across the land,
Land that once was beautiful
Now was left derelict and uninhabited.

Deafened by the thunderous roar,
Survivors crouched in the ruins
Which once were their homes,
Devastation was all that the tornado left behind.

Kay Llewellyn (13)

THERE'S A MONSTER UNDER MY BED

Last night when I was in my bed
I knew I would get a fright,
When my mum came in and said,
I'm turning off the light.

I heard a gnawing, crunching sound
Coming from below my head
I felt my heart begin to pound
There's a monster under my bed.

I grabbed a stone from my side
I tried to hit its head
I quickly, quickly tried to hide
There's a monster under my bed.

Laura Wilkins (12)

The Darkness Of Fear

Fear, a fear of being afraid
A fear of panic and one of worry
A fear of doubt and pain
To dread is to be afraid, to fear.

The sweat of fear ascending from the forehead
As the fright sets in
The uneasiness of terror as fear approaches
Then fear strikes a powerful blow
Fear then decimates the body.

The body now destroyed, the heartbeat showing
Now the attempt at recovery begins
The fear now over the dark turns to light
The dread of fear returns to the depths of hell.

Michael Patterson (13)

The Gathering Of Death

Dark, an aura of darkness covers the scene and
a stench of rotten air fills the room.
The gathering was filled with both men and
women, their faces white as ghosts in the shadow
of the moon.
All men and women had the looks of children but
the wisdom of owls.
All looked like cold stone statues without a heart
The only sign of emotion was a single tear rolling
down the cold cheek.
The only movement was a single finger brushing
away the isolated tear and all expressions were lost.
The face was like a tombstone with no inscription.

Philip Wilson (14)

MASKS OF MEMORY

Masks, spinning, twirling.
Blood, flowing, crawling.
Masks, leering, jeering.
Crimson, blood-red!
My masks.
The masks I give unto myself.
Masks of shroud.
A shroud of lies to hide the truth.
Obscure and faded.
Shrouds and masks corrupted.
And so abandoned for new ones.
New masks, new shrouds.
To hide old lies and old hate.
Dreams of flesh and steel.
To hide the one terrible truth.
That truth cannot be hidden.
Or banished.
Not by lies.
Not by hate.
Nor by walls, violence or faded masks.
And the bottom line.
Lies, truths, memories, those little things we would all rather
Forget, are always there.
Masks and shrouds fade, and rot.
But the memory remains.

Dominic Sewell (14)

FOLLOWER

(After Seamus Heaney)

My father worked with all boilers,
His mind, a mechanical clock.
Amongst the pumps and back oil
The burners lit when the match was struck.

An expert. He would test the flame
As the pilot light used to choke.
He turned the dial just a grain, so that
It started not even with a cough of smoke.

I stood in his way in the outhouse
And rarely turned on the right switch.
Sometimes I'd carry his toolbox,
But never knew which tool was which.

I wanted to be like my dad,
To mend all the boilers with ease,
But my mind fought against what my dad's had
So I just stood and admired his speed.

I was a nuisance, not understanding,
Plodding behind him, asking him why.
Today though the story is changing
As I set the pace for him to try.

Jen Dyer (15)

THE LITTLE GREEN MAN

There is a little green man who sits in the garden
He sits there staring at me
'Come with me, come with me,' he says loudly
But I don't, I just run and hide.

No one else can see or hear him
They just think that I'm going mad
But I don't think I'm really too bad
Because he sits there staring at me.

I tried to run away one day
But he followed me wherever I went
I couldn't get away so I decided to stay
And he sits there staring at me.

That little green man really does frighten me
When he stares at me with those big blue eyes
I try to look away but wherever I look
He is sitting there staring at me.

One day some people came to take me away
They wouldn't tell me where I was going
But I would be free from the little green man
Who sits there staring at me.

I went with the people and sat in their car
I sat in the back and strapped myself up
And who did I see just sitting next to me?
That little green man just staring at me.

Adam Spoors (13)

VOLCANO

A volcano sleeping under a blanket of ice
All is normal, a quiet mountain
Hundreds of years since its last destruction
Just biding its time and waiting to explode.

Loud rumbling deafens nearby villages
Screaming and shouting as people are fleeing
But some people cannot leave their village behind
Highly risking their lives at a fatal cost.

The lava rises from inside the mountain
Boiling hot lava shoots up into the sky
As the molten rock rises over the brim
And rushes down the side of the dangerous mountain.

Fire crackers go off like on bonfire night
But this noise sounds a million times greater
Red hot ashes and dust start filling the air
As this sea of dark clouds turns the sky pitch black.

Lava flows like menacing sea serpents
Falling rocks are eaten up by these flows
Poisonous gases start spreading in the air
Blizzards of fire start lining the sky.

This powerful destruction carries on for days
Falls of lava and fire rushes down to the villages
Curtains of fire and glowing clouds die down
As the heat of this lava cools down very slowly.

Mudslides now come and cause another threat
Like quicksand it swallows anything it can find
As people start to rebuild their desolate village
The volcano builds up and will strike again.

Alexander MacGregor (12)

I Wish . . .

I wish, I wish, I wish
for a horse, a dog, a rabbit
but I have a cat instead.

I wish, I wish, I wish
for all the sweets in the world,
but I have a birthday cake.

I wish, I wish, I wish
my brothers could be my slaves
but they are nothing but annoying.

I wish, I wish, I wish
for a mansion and a limo
but I have a pink house and an estate.

I wish, I wish, I wish
really hard on my birthday.

Eloise Pearce (14)

FARM FEVER
(With apologies to John Masefield)

I must go down to the farm again, to the chicken-coop and the sty,
And all I ask is a horse and cart and a whip to steer it by,
And the wheel's kick and the wife's song and the brown cart's shaking,
And a blue haze on the hill's face and a grey dawn breaking.

I must get down to the farm again, to my hard-working life,
To the sweet hay and lamb's play and the sweet song of my wife;
And all I ask is a sickle, and fresh ripe corn to reap,
And the daily sight of steam, rising off the horses' muck heap.

I must get down to the farm again, for the horses are in foal,
My checking them at three a.m. is beginning to take its toll;
And all I ask is a horse's stall that needs to be mucked out,
A farmer's life is the best life, of that there is no doubt.

Ruth Gripper (12)

BALLYMONEY

Three children rest still,
Together in charcoal-choked beds,
The smell of fired flesh oozes from them,
Hanging in the hollow of my head.

Teeth revealed from under bacon-curled lips,
They snarl back at me; hungry,
Straining for some final sacred sight,
Their poached eyes stare out, beyond me.

They remain a Trinity of religious construction,
Or Holy relics, evidence from old,
'Bible-black' the skin peels from them,
Uncovering white-paged souls.

Ben Martin (18)

LITTLE PUMPKIN

The clock struck twelve
November the first
And the little pumpkin shed a tear.
It was too late for him now
His destiny unfulfilled.
His whole life he'd waited for this one day,
Hallowe'en.

How he'd longed to be a child's lantern
To be given a face, an identity,
Not just another pumpkin in the crowd.

On the shelf in the shop
He'd stood up tall
Picked up and squeezed,
'Yes! I'm going home!'
Then put back down.
Never mind, here comes another,
And another . . .

Days pass,
Pumpkins come and go.
Little pumpkin a little bruised
A little worse for wear.
No one wants a little pumpkin.

And the little pumpkin knows,
At the strike of the clock,
That his destiny is no longer
To become something special
But to be thrown on the compost heap.

Bex Spence (17)

LESSONS AT WAR

Geography is often plotting points,
To give Physics an electric shock.
It gives Maths many problems, but
For English it's as easy as ABC.

'A Civil War!' History cried,
To this, Music sang.
'Look out! DT is hurling planes!'
'Encore!' Foreign Languages replied.

'How thrilling!' exclaimed Drama,
'A true epic!' RE replied.
Biology arrived amoebic-like
While Chemistry bubbled into action.

PE and Games came rushing by,
Yet Art took time to picture.
IT went 'Information overload!'
But Ceramics threw in the wheel.

Then the Head emerged from his study.
'Get back to work!' he yelled.
But Geography is still plotting points,
To give Physics an electric shock . . . !

Rachael O'Rourke

BUT MY FRIEND HAD NONE

Forgotten Dictionary

Writing a poem without a dictionary is like:

> Yelling without shouting,
> Cooking without heat,
>   or
> Reading without text,
>
> So my friend lent me one.

Forgotten Paper

Writing a poem without some paper is like:

> Shooting without a gun,
> Counting without numbers,
>   or
> Sailing without a boat,
>
> So my friend lent me some.

Forgotten Pencil

Writing a poem without a pencil is like:

> Writing on air,
> Plastering on paper,
>   or
> Gardening on concrete,
>
> So my friend lent me one.

The next thing I noticed was that my best friend had no:
> Dictionary
> Paper
> or even a pencil.

John Badcock (11)

I DON'T KNOW WHAT TO SAY TO HER

If I were to swim with a shark,
I'd make sure it would bite me;
Sticks and stones may break my bones,
But 'gale-force eight' excites me.
I said all this just for a kiss,
But I don't think she likes me.
I tried to tell her pace by pace,
But ended up with a slap in the face.
I like to eat a bit of meat,
But really, I'm not fat.
But when I tried to tell her this,
She said I am a brat.
Maybe if girls had no brains,
And no hands for slaps;
The blokes inside this tiny world
Would be more happy chaps.

Ben Maling